comfort food

comfort food

Kay Scarlett

LAUREL
GLEN
San Diego, California

Contents

Soups

Shrimp gumbo

2 tablespoons olive oil
1 large onion, finely chopped
3 garlic cloves, crushed
1 red bell pepper, chopped
4 slices bacon, chopped
1 1/2 teaspoons dried thyme
2 teaspoons dried oregano
1 teaspoon paprika
1/2 teaspoon cayenne pepper
1/4 cup sherry
4 cups fish stock
1/2 cup long-grain rice
2 bay leaves
14 oz. can diced tomatoes
1/4 lb. okra, trimmed and thinly sliced
2 lb. medium shrimp, peeled and
  deveined
3 tablespoons finely chopped Italian
  parsley

Heat the oil in a large saucepan over low heat. Cook the onion, garlic, pepper, and bacon for 5 minutes or until soft. Stir in the herbs and spices. Season. Add the sherry and cook until evaporated, then add the stock and 2 cups water. Bring to a boil. Add the rice and bay leaves, reduce the heat, and simmer, covered, for 20 minutes.

Add the tomatoes and okra. Simmer, covered, for 20–25 minutes. Stir in the shrimp and parsley and simmer for 5 minutes or until the shrimp are cooked through.

Serves 4

Butternut squash and carrot soup

3 tablespoons butter
1 large onion, chopped
2 garlic cloves, crushed
1 lb. carrots, sliced
$1/2$ cup orange juice
$1^3/4$ lb. butternut squash, peeled
  and roughly chopped
6 cups chicken stock
1 tablespoon snipped chives
herb scones or herb bread, to serve

Melt the butter in a large saucepan over medium heat and cook the onion for 5 minutes or until soft and starting to brown. Add the garlic and carrots and cook for another 5 minutes or until starting to soften. Pour in the orange juice and bring to a boil over high heat. Add the squash, stock, and 2 cups water and return to a boil. Reduce the heat and simmer for 30 minutes or until the carrots and squash are soft.

Blend the soup in batches in a blender until smooth—add a little more stock if you prefer the soup to be a thinner consistency.

Return to the cleaned pan and reheat. Season to taste with salt and freshly ground pepper. Divide the soup among serving bowls and garnish with the chives. Serve with herb scones or bread.

Serves 4–6

Broiled Italian sausage and vegetable soup

1 lb. Italian pork sausages
7 oz. piece cured smoked ham
1 tablespoon olive oil
1 large onion, chopped
3 garlic cloves, crushed
1 celery stalk, cut in half and sliced
1 large carrot, cut into 1/2 inch cubes
bouquet garni (1 parsley sprig,
   1 oregano sprig, 2 bay leaves)
1 small red chili, halved lengthwise
14 oz. can diced tomatoes
7 cups chicken stock
3/4 lb. Brussels sprouts, cut in half
   from top to bottom
3/4 lb. green beans, cut into 1 1/4 inch
   pieces
3/4 lb. shelled fava beans, fresh
   or canned
2 tablespoons chopped Italian parsley

Broil the sausages under a preheated broiler for 8–10 minutes, turning occasionally, until brown. Remove and cut into 1 1/4 inch pieces. Trim and reserve the fat from the ham, then dice the ham.

Heat the oil in a large saucepan over medium heat. Add the ham and reserved ham fat and cook for 2–3 minutes or until golden. Add the onion, garlic, celery, and carrot, reduce the heat to low, and cook for 6–8 minutes or until softened. Discard the remains of the ham fat.

Stir in the sausages, bouquet garni, chili, and diced tomato and cook for 5 minutes. Add the stock, bring to a boil, then reduce the heat and simmer for 1 hour. Add the Brussels sprouts, green beans, and fava beans and simmer for 30 minutes. Discard the bouquet garni, then stir in the parsley. Season to taste. Divide among four bowls and serve.

Serves 4

Leek and potato soup

3½ tablespoons butter
1 onion, finely chopped
3 leeks, white part only, sliced
1 celery stalk, finely chopped
1 garlic clove, finely chopped
½ lb. potatoes, chopped
3 cups chicken stock
¾ cup light whipping cream
2 tablespoons chopped chives

Melt the butter in a large saucepan and add the onion, leeks, celery, and garlic. Cover the saucepan and cook, stirring occasionally, over low heat for 15 minutes or until the vegetables are softened but not browned. Add the potatoes and stock and bring to a boil.

Reduce the heat and allow to simmer, covered, for 20 minutes. Allow the soup to cool a little before puréeing in a blender or food processor. Return to the cleaned saucepan.

Bring the soup gently back to a boil and stir in the cream. Season with salt and white pepper and reheat without boiling. Serve hot or well chilled, garnished with chives.

Serves 6

Tomato and bread soup

1³/₄ lb. vine-ripened tomatoes
1 lb. loaf day-old crusty Italian bread
1 tablespoon olive oil
3 garlic cloves, crushed
1 tablespoon tomato paste
5 cups hot vegetable stock
4 tablespoons torn basil leaves
2–3 tablespoons extra-virgin olive oil,
  plus extra, to serve

Score a cross in the base of each tomato. Place in a bowl of boiling water for 1 minute, then plunge into cold water and peel the skin away from the cross. Cut the tomatoes in half and scoop out the seeds with a teaspoon. Chop the tomato flesh.

Remove most of the crust from the bread and discard. Cut the bread into 1¹/₄ inch pieces.

Heat the oil in a large saucepan. Add the garlic, tomatoes, and tomato paste, then reduce the heat and simmer, stirring occasionally, for 15 minutes or until thickened. Add the stock and bring to a boil, stirring, for 2 minutes. Reduce the heat to medium, add the bread pieces, and cook, stirring, for 5 minutes or until the bread softens and absorbs most of the liquid. Add more stock or water if necessary.

Stir in the torn basil leaves and extra-virgin olive oil and leave for 5 minutes so the flavors have time to develop. Drizzle with a little of the extra oil.

Serves 4

Note: This soup is popular in Italy in the summer months when tomatoes are at their tastiest, and as a way of using up leftover bread. In Italy, the soup is called *Pappa al pomodoro*.

Asparagus soup with Parmesan crisps

1 1/2 lb. fresh asparagus, trimmed
1 tablespoon vegetable oil
2 tablespoons butter
1 large red onion, finely chopped
1 large leek, thinly sliced
2 large potatoes, cut into 1/2 inch
  cubes
5 cups chicken stock
1/3 cup light whipping cream
1/3 cup sour cream
1 tablespoon snipped chives
2/3 cup grated Parmesan cheese

Roughly chop 1 lb. 7 oz. of the asparagus and cut the rest into 2 1/2 inch pieces. Heat the oil and butter in a large saucepan over medium heat and cook the onion and leek for 5 minutes or until soft. Add the potatoes, chopped asparagus, and chicken stock and bring to a boil over high heat. Reduce the heat and simmer for 8 minutes or until the vegetables are tender. Blanch the remaining asparagus in a saucepan of boiling water.

Cool the soup, then purée. Return to the saucepan and stir in the cream for 1–2 minutes or until heated through. Season. Garnish with sour cream, the blanched asparagus, and chives.

To make the Parmesan crisps, preheat the oven to 375°F. Line three greased cookie sheets with baking paper and place four 3 1/2 inch egg rings on each cookie sheet. Divide the Parmesan into three portions. Sprinkle one portion evenly into the four rings in a thin layer. Repeat with remaining portions of Parmesan to make twelve cups. For a lacy edge, remove the rings. Bake for 5 minutes or until melted and just golden brown. Allow to cool and serve with the soup.

Serves 4

Chicken laksa

Chicken balls
1 lb. ground chicken
1 small red chili, finely chopped
2 garlic cloves, finely chopped
½ small red onion, finely chopped
1 lemongrass stalk (white part only),
   finely chopped
2 tablespoons chopped cilantro

7 oz. dried rice vermicelli
1 tablespoon peanut oil
¼ cup good-quality laksa paste
4 cups chicken stock
2 cups coconut milk
8 fried tofu puffs, cut in half diagonally
1 cup bean sprouts
2 tablespoons shredded Vietnamese
   mint
3 tablespoons shredded cilantro
lime wedges, to serve
fish sauce, to serve (optional)

To make the balls, process all the ingredients in a food processor until just combined. Roll tablespoons of the mixture into balls with wet hands.

Place the vermicelli in a heatproof bowl, cover with boiling water, and soak for 6–7 minutes. Drain well.

Heat the oil in a large saucepan over medium heat. Add the laksa paste and cook for 1–2 minutes or until aromatic. Add the stock, reduce the heat, and simmer for 10 minutes. Add the coconut milk and chicken balls and simmer for 5 minutes or until the balls are cooked through.

Divide the vermicelli, tofu puffs, and bean sprouts among four serving bowls and ladle the soup over the top, dividing the balls evenly. Garnish with the mint and cilantro. Serve with the lime wedges and fish sauce.

Serves 4

Note: Laksa paste is often used as a base for soups. It is available from Asian markets.

Ravioli broth with lemon and baby spinach

Stock

3¹/₄ lb. chicken bones (necks, backs, wings)
2 large leeks, chopped
2 large carrots, chopped
2 large celery stalks, chopped
6 lemon thyme sprigs
4 sprigs Italian parsley
10 black peppercorns

12 oz. fresh veal ravioli
2 strips lemon zest (2½ inches long), white pith removed
¹/₄ lb. baby spinach leaves, stems removed
¹/₂ teaspoon lemon oil
1–2 tablespoons lemon juice
¹/₃ cup shaved Parmesan cheese, to garnish

Place the chicken bones in a large saucepan with 12 cups cold water. Bring to a simmer over medium-low heat (do not boil) for 30 minutes, removing any foam that rises to the surface. Add the remaining stock ingredients and simmer, partially covered, for 3 hours. Pass through a fine strainer and cool. Cover and refrigerate overnight. Remove the layer of fat on the surface.

Place the stock in a large saucepan and bring to a boil. Add the ravioli and zest and cook for 3–5 minutes or until the ravioli floats to the top and is tender. Stir in the spinach and season. Discard the zest, and just before serving, stir in the lemon oil (to taste) and lemon juice. Garnish with the shaved Parmesan.

Serves 4

Lentil and vegetable soup with spiced yogurt

2 tablespoons olive oil
1 small leek (white part only), chopped
2 garlic cloves, crushed
2 teaspoons curry powder
1 teaspoon ground cumin
1 teaspoon garam masala
4 cups vegetable stock
1 fresh bay leaf
1 cup brown lentils
1 lb. butternut squash, peeled and cut into 1/2 inch cubes
14 oz. can diced tomatoes
2 zucchini, cut in half lengthwise and sliced
1/2 lb. broccoli, cut into small florets
1 small carrot, diced
1/2 cup peas
1 tablespoon chopped mint

Spiced yogurt
1 cup plain yogurt
1 tablespoon chopped cilantro
1 garlic clove, crushed
3 dashes hot pepper sauce

Heat the oil in a saucepan over medium heat. Add the leek and garlic and cook for 4–5 minutes or until soft and lightly golden. Add the curry powder, cumin, and garam masala and cook for 1 minute or until the spices are fragrant.

Add the stock, bay leaf, lentils, and butternut squash. Bring to a boil, then reduce the heat to low and simmer for 10–15 minutes or until the lentils are tender. Season well.

Add the tomatoes, zucchini, broccoli, carrot, and 2 cups water and simmer for 10 minutes or until the vegetables are tender. Add the peas and simmer for 2–3 minutes.

To make the spiced yogurt, place the yogurt, cilantro, garlic, and hot pepper sauce in a small bowl and stir until combined. Spoon a dollop of the yogurt on each serving of soup and garnish with the chopped mint.

Serves 6

Pork congee

1 1/2 cups long-grain rice, thoroughly
  rinsed
1/2 star anise
2 scallions, white part only
1 1/2 x 1 1/2 inch piece ginger, cut
  into slices
14 cups chicken stock
1 tablespoon peanut oil
2 garlic cloves, crushed
1 teaspoon grated ginger, extra
14 oz. ground pork
ground white pepper
1/4 cup light soy sauce
sesame oil, to drizzle
6 fried dough sticks (see Note)

Put the rice in a large saucepan with
the star anise, scallions, sliced ginger,
and chicken stock. Bring to a boil, then
reduce the heat to low and simmer for
1 1/2 hours, stirring occasionally.

Heat the oil in a frying pan over high
heat. Cook the garlic and grated
ginger for 30 seconds. Add the
ground pork and cook for 5 minutes
or until browned, breaking up any
lumps with the back of a spoon.

Remove the star anise, scallions, and
ginger from the soup and discard
them. Add the pork mixture and
simmer for 10 minutes. Season with
white pepper and stir in the soy
sauce. Serve with a drizzle of sesame
oil and the dough sticks.

Serves 4–6

Note: Fried dough sticks are available
at Asian markets and are best eaten
soon after purchase. Otherwise,
reheat the dough sticks in a 400°F
oven for 5 minutes, then serve.

Zucchini soup

1/4 cup butter
2 large leeks (white part only), thinly
sliced
4 garlic cloves, crushed
2³/₄ lb. zucchini, coarsely grated
7 cups chicken stock
1/3 cup light whipping cream
bacon and onion bread, to serve
(optional)

Melt the butter in a saucepan over medium heat. Cook the leeks, stirring once or twice, for 2–3 minutes or until they start to soften. Reduce the heat to low, add the garlic, and cook, covered, stirring once or twice, for 10 minutes or until the leeks are really soft—do not allow them to brown.

Add the zucchini to the saucepan and cook, uncovered, for 4–5 minutes. Pour in the chicken stock and bring to a boil over high heat. Reduce the heat to medium-low and simmer for 20 minutes or until soft.

Let the soup cool slightly, then blend half in a blender until smooth. Return to the saucepan, stir in the whipping cream, and gently reheat over medium heat until warmed through. Season to taste with salt and freshly ground black pepper. Serve the soup with bacon and onion bread or fresh, crusty bread, if desired.

Serves 4

Orange sweet potato soup

3 tablespoons butter
2 onions, chopped
2 garlic cloves, crushed
2¼ lb. orange sweet potatoes, peeled
  and chopped
1 large celery stalk, chopped
1 large green apple, peeled, cored,
  and chopped
1½ teaspoons ground cumin
8 cups chicken stock
½ cup plain yogurt
lavash bread, to serve (optional)

Melt the butter in a large saucepan over low heat. Add the onions and cook, stirring occasionally, for 10 minutes or until soft. Add the garlic, sweet potatoes, celery, apple, and 1 teaspoon of the cumin and continue to cook for 5–7 minutes or until well coated. Add the chicken stock and the remaining cumin and bring to a boil over high heat. Reduce the heat and simmer for 25–30 minutes or until the sweet potatoes are very soft.

Cool the soup slightly and blend in batches until smooth. Return to the cleaned saucepan and gently stir over medium heat until warmed through. Season with salt and freshly ground black pepper. Divide among serving bowls and top each serving with a dollop of yogurt.

Cut the lavash bread into rectangular strips, brush lightly with oil, and place on a cookie sheet. Bake in a 375°F oven for 15–20 minutes or until crisp and lightly golden. Serve with the soup.

Serves 4–6

Chicken, mushroom, and Madeira soup

1/4 oz. dried porcini mushrooms
1 tablespoon butter
1 leek (white part only), thinly sliced
9 oz. pancetta or bacon, chopped
1/2 lb. portobello mushrooms, roughly
  chopped
3/4 lb. large field mushrooms, roughly
  chopped
2 tablespoons all-purpose flour
1/2 cup Madeira
5 cups chicken stock
1 tablespoon olive oil
2 boneless, skinless chicken breasts
  (about 7 oz. each)
1/3 cup light sour cream
2 teaspoons chopped marjoram
whole marjoram leaves, extra, to
  garnish

Soak the porcini mushrooms in 1 cup boiling water for 20 minutes.

Melt the butter in a large saucepan over medium heat and cook the leek and pancetta for 5 minutes or until the leek is softened. Add all the mushrooms and the porcini soaking liquid and cook for 10 minutes.

Stir in the flour and cook for 1 minute. Add the Madeira and cook, stirring, for 10 minutes. Stir in the stock, bring to a boil, then reduce the heat and simmer for 45 minutes. Cool slightly.

Heat the oil in a frying pan and cook the chicken breasts for 4–5 minutes each side or until cooked through. Remove from the pan and thinly slice.

Blend the soup until smooth. Return to the cleaned saucepan, add the sour cream and chopped marjoram, and stir over medium heat for about 1–2 minutes to warm through. Season. Top with the chicken and garnish with the marjoram leaves.

Serves 4

Long and short noodle soup

10½ oz. ground pork
4 scallions, sliced
3 garlic cloves, roughly chopped
2 teaspoons grated ginger
2 teaspoons cornstarch
½ cup light soy sauce
3 tablespoons Chinese rice wine
30 wonton wrappers
12 cups store-bought Chinese
  chicken broth, or homemade or
  store-bought chicken stock
7 oz. dried flat egg noodles
2 scallions, extra, sliced diagonally
1 teaspoon sesame oil

Put the ground pork, scallions, garlic, grated ginger, cornstarch, 1½ tablespoons of the soy sauce, and 1 tablespoon of the rice wine in a food processor and process until well combined. Place 2 teaspoons of the mixture in the center of a wonton wrapper and lightly brush the edges with water. Lift the sides up tightly and pinch around the filling to form a pouch. Repeat this process to make thirty wontons.

Place the chicken broth in a large saucepan and bring to a simmer over medium-high heat. Stir in the remaining soy sauce and rice wine.

Meanwhile, bring a large saucepan of water to a boil. Reduce the heat, add the wontons, and simmer for 1 minute or until they float to the surface and are cooked through, then remove with a slotted spoon. Return the water to a boil, add the egg noodles, and cook for 3 minutes or until tender. Drain and add to the chicken broth along with the cooked wontons. Simmer for 2 minutes or until heated through.

Divide the broth, noodles, and wontons among six large serving bowls, sprinkle with extra scallions, and lightly drizzle with sesame oil.

Serves 6

Chickpea soup with spiced pita bread

1 tablespoon olive oil
1 large onion, chopped
5 garlic cloves, chopped
1 large carrot, chopped
1 bay leaf
2 celery stalks, chopped
1 teaspoon ground cumin
$\frac{1}{2}$ teaspoon ground cinnamon
15 oz. can chickpeas, drained and
    rinsed
5 cups chicken stock
1 tablespoon finely chopped Italian
    parsley, plus extra, to garnish
1 tablespoon finely chopped cilantro
2 tablespoons lemon juice
extra-virgin olive oil, to drizzle

Spiced pita bread
3 tablespoons butter
2 tablespoons olive oil
2 garlic cloves, crushed
$\frac{1}{8}$ teaspoon ground cumin
$\frac{1}{8}$ teaspoon ground cinnamon
$\frac{1}{8}$ teaspoon cayenne pepper
$\frac{1}{2}$ teaspoon sea salt
4 small pita breads, split

Heat the oil in a large saucepan and cook the onion over medium heat for 3–4 minutes or until soft. Add the garlic, carrot, bay leaf, and celery and cook for 4 minutes or until the vegetables start to caramelize.

Stir in the cumin and cinnamon and cook for 1 minute. Add the chickpeas, stock, and 4 cups water and bring to a boil. Reduce the heat and simmer for 1 hour. Allow to cool.

Remove the bay leaf and purée the soup. Return to the cleaned pan and stir over medium heat until warmed. Stir in the herbs and lemon juice. Season. Drizzle with oil and garnish with parsley.

To make the spiced pita bread, melt the butter and oil in a saucepan over medium heat. Add the garlic, spices, and salt and cook for 1 minute. Place the pita, smooth side up, on a lined baking sheet and toast for 1–2 minutes or until golden. Turn and brush with the spiced butter. Toast until golden and serve with the soup.

Serves 4–6

Creamy chicken and corn soup

1 tablespoon butter
1 tablespoon olive oil
1 lb. boneless, skinless chicken
  thighs, trimmed and thinly sliced
2 garlic cloves, chopped
1 leek, chopped
1 large celery stalk, chopped
1 bay leaf
½ teaspoon thyme
4 cups chicken stock
¼ cup sherry
1¼ lb. corn kernels (fresh, canned,
  or frozen)
1 large russet potato, cut into
  ½ inch cubes
¾ cup light whipping cream, plus
  extra, to drizzle
chives, to garnish

Melt the butter and oil in a large saucepan over high heat. Cook the chicken in batches for 3 minutes or until lightly golden and just cooked through. Place in a bowl, cover, and refrigerate until needed.

Reduce the heat to medium and stir in the garlic, leek, celery, bay leaf, and thyme. Cook for 2 minutes or until the leek softens—do not allow the garlic to burn. Add the stock, sherry, and 2 cups water and stir, scraping up any sediment stuck to the bottom of the saucepan. Add the corn and potato and bring to a boil. Reduce the heat and simmer for 1 hour, skimming any foam off the surface. Cool slightly.

Remove the bay leaf and purée the soup. Return to the cleaned pan, add the cream and chicken, and stir over medium-low heat for 2–3 minutes or until heated through—do not boil. Season. Drizzle with extra cream and garnish with chives. If desired, serve with crusty bread.

Serves 4–6

Duck, shiitake mushroom, and rice noodle broth

3 dried shiitake mushrooms
1 roast duck (3¼ lb.)
2 cups chicken stock
2 tablespoons light soy sauce
1 tablespoon Chinese rice wine
2 teaspoons sugar
14 oz. fresh flat rice noodles
2 tablespoons vegetable oil
3 scallions, thinly sliced
1 teaspoon finely chopped ginger
1 lb. bok choy, trimmed and leaves
    separated
¼ teaspoon sesame oil

Place the mushrooms in a heatproof bowl, cover with 1 cup boiling water, and soak for 20 minutes. Drain, reserving the liquid and squeezing the excess liquid from the mushrooms. Discard the woody stems and thinly slice the caps.

Remove the skin and flesh from the roast duck. Discard the fat and carcass. Finely slice the duck meat and the skin.

Place the chicken stock, soy sauce, rice wine, sugar, and the reserved mushroom liquid in a saucepan over medium heat. Bring to a simmer and cook for 5 minutes. Meanwhile, place the rice noodles in a heatproof bowl, cover with boiling water, and soak briefly. Gently separate the noodles with your hands and drain well. Divide evenly among large soup bowls.

Heat the oil in a wok over high heat. Add the scallions, ginger, and shiitake mushrooms and cook for several seconds. Transfer to the broth with the bok choy and duck meat and simmer for 1 minute or until the duck has warmed through and the bok choy has wilted. Ladle the soup over the noodles and drizzle sesame oil on each serving. Serve immediately.

Serves 4–6

Avgolemono with chicken

1 carrot, chopped
1 large leek, chopped
2 bay leaves
2 boneless, skinless chicken breasts
8 cups chicken stock
1/3 cup short-grain rice
3 eggs, separated
1/3 cup lemon juice
2 tablespoons chopped parsley
3 tablespoons butter, chopped

Place the carrot, leek, bay leaves, chicken breasts, and stock in a large saucepan. Bring to a boil over high heat, then reduce the heat and simmer for 10–15 minutes or until the chicken is cooked. Strain into a clean saucepan and reserve the chicken.

Add the rice to the liquid, bring to a boil, then reduce the heat and simmer for 15 minutes or until tender. Cut the chicken into 1/2 inch cubes.

Whisk the egg whites in a clean, dry bowl until firm peaks form. Beat in the yolks until light and creamy, whisk in the lemon juice, then 1 cup of the soup. Remove the soup from the heat and gradually whisk in the egg mixture. Add the chicken and stir over low heat for 2 minutes—do not boil or the egg will scramble. Serve at once with a sprinkle of parsley and a pat of butter.

Serves 4

Note: This soup should be made just before serving.

Spaghetti and meatball soup

5½ oz. spaghetti, broken into 3 inch
  pieces
6 cups beef stock
3 teaspoons tomato paste
14 oz. can diced tomatoes
3 tablespoons basil leaves, torn
shaved Parmesan cheese, to garnish

Meatballs
1 tablespoon oil
1 onion, finely chopped
2 garlic cloves, crushed
1 lb. lean ground beef
3 tablespoons finely chopped Italian
  parsley
3 tablespoons fresh bread crumbs
2 tablespoons finely grated Parmesan
  cheese
1 egg, lightly beaten

Cook the spaghetti in a large
saucepan of boiling water according
to package instructions until al dente.
Drain. Put the stock and 2 cups water
in a large saucepan and slowly bring
to a simmer.

Meanwhile, to make the meatballs,
heat the oil in a small frying pan over
medium heat and cook the onion for
2–3 minutes or until soft. Add the
garlic and cook for 30 seconds.
Allow to cool.

Combine the ground beef, parsley,
bread crumbs, Parmesan, egg, onion
mixture, and salt and pepper. Roll a
heaping teaspoon of mixture into a
ball, making forty balls.

Stir the tomato paste and tomatoes
into the beef stock and simmer for
2–3 minutes. Drop in the meatballs,
return to a simmer, and cook for
10 minutes or until cooked through.
Stir in the spaghetti and basil to warm
through. Season, garnish with shaved
Parmesan, and serve.

Serves 4

Cabbage soup

½ cup dried navy beans
4½ oz. bacon, cubed
3 tablespoons butter
1 carrot, sliced
1 onion, chopped
1 leek, white part only, roughly
  chopped
1 turnip, peeled and chopped
bouquet garni
5 cups chicken stock
¾ lb. white cabbage, finely shredded

Soak the beans overnight in cold water. Drain, put in a saucepan, and cover with cold water. Bring to a boil and simmer for 5 minutes, then drain. Put the bacon in the same saucepan, cover with water, and simmer for 5 minutes. Drain and pat dry with paper towels.

Melt the butter in a large, heavy-bottomed saucepan, add the bacon, and cook for 5 minutes without browning. Add the beans, carrot, onion, leek, and turnip and cook for 5 minutes. Add the bouquet garni and chicken stock and bring to a boil. Cover and simmer for 30 minutes. Add the cabbage, uncover, and simmer for 30 minutes or until the beans are tender. Remove the bouquet garni before serving and season to taste.

Serves 4

Spicy seafood and roasted corn soup

2 corncobs (1 1/2 lb.)
1 tablespoon olive oil
1 red onion, finely chopped
1 small red chili, finely chopped
1/2 teaspoon ground allspice
4 vine-ripened tomatoes, peeled and
 finely diced
6 cups fish stock or light chicken
 stock
10 1/2 oz. firm, boneless white fish
 fillets (cod, halibut, or perch), diced
7 oz. fresh crabmeat
7 oz. peeled shrimp, roughly chopped
1 tablespoon lime juice

Quesadillas
4 flour tortillas (7 1/2 inch)
2/3 cup grated cheddar cheese
4 tablespoons cilantro
2 tablespoons olive oil

Preheat the oven to 400°F. Peel back the husks on the corncobs (making sure they stay intact at the base) and remove the silks. Fold the husks back over the corn, place in a baking dish, and bake for 1 hour or until the cobs are tender.

Heat the oil in a large saucepan over medium heat. Add the onion and cook until soft. Add the chili and allspice and cook for 1 minute, then add the tomatoes and stock and bring to a boil. Reduce the heat and simmer, covered, for 45 minutes.

Slice the kernels from the cobs with a sharp knife, add to the soup, and simmer, uncovered, for 15 minutes. Add the fish, crab, and shrimp meat to the soup and simmer for 5 minutes or until the seafood is cooked. Stir in the lime juice and serve with the quesadillas, if desired.

To make the quesadillas, top one tortilla with half the cheese and half the cilantro. Season, then top with another tortilla. Heat 1 tablespoon of the oil in a frying pan and cook the quesadilla for 30 seconds on each side or until the cheese just begins to melt. Repeat to make the other quesadilla. Cut into wedges.

Serves 4

Vietnamese beef soup

14 oz. rump steak, trimmed
1/2 onion
1 1/2 tablespoons fish sauce
1 star anise
1 cinnamon stick
pinch ground white pepper
6 cups beef stock
10 1/2 oz. fresh thin rice noodles
3 scallions, thinly sliced
3/4 cup Vietnamese mint leaves
1 cup bean sprouts
1 small white onion, cut in half and
thinly sliced
1 small red chili, thinly sliced
diagonally
lemon wedges, to serve

Wrap the rump steak in plastic wrap and freeze for 40 minutes.

Meanwhile, put the onion, fish sauce, star anise, cinnamon stick, pepper, stock, and 2 cups water in a large saucepan. Bring to a boil, then reduce the heat, cover, and simmer for 20 minutes. Discard the onion, star anise, and cinnamon stick.

Cover the noodles with boiling water and gently separate the strands. Drain and rinse under cold water.

Remove the meat from the freezer and thinly slice it across the grain.

Divide the noodles and scallions among four deep bowls. Top with the beef, mint, bean sprouts, onion, and chili. Ladle the hot broth over the top and serve with the lemon wedges.

Serves 4

Note: In Vietnam, noodle soups are called *pho*; beef noodle soup, *pho bo*, is one of the most popular.

Minestrone

1 cup dried borlotti beans
3½ tablespoons butter
1 large onion, finely chopped
1 garlic clove, finely chopped
¾ cup parsley, finely chopped
2 sage leaves
3½ oz. pancetta or bacon, cubed
2 celery stalks, halved, then sliced
2 carrots, sliced
3 potatoes, peeled but left whole
1 teaspoon tomato paste
14 oz. can diced tomatoes
8 basil leaves
12 cups chicken or vegetable stock
2 zucchini, sliced
1⅓ cups shelled peas
¼ lb. scarlet runner beans, cut into
   1½ inch pieces
¼ cabbage, shredded
5½ oz. ditalini, avemarie, or other
   small pasta
grated Parmesan cheese, to serve

Pesto
2 garlic cloves, crushed
⅓ cup pine nuts
1¾ cups firmly packed basil leaves
4 tablespoons grated Parmesan
   cheese
½ cup extra-virgin olive oil

Put the dried borlotti beans in a large bowl, cover with cold water, and allow to soak overnight. Drain and rinse under cold water.

Melt the butter in a saucepan and add the onion, garlic, parsley, sage, and pancetta. Cook over low heat, stirring once or twice, for 10 minutes or until the onion is soft and golden.

Add the celery, carrots, and potatoes and cook for 5 minutes. Stir in the tomato paste, tomatoes, basil, and dried beans. Season with plenty of pepper. Add the stock and bring slowly to a boil. Cover and allow to simmer for 2 hours, stirring once or twice.

If the potatoes haven't already broken up, roughly break them up with a fork against the side of the saucepan. Taste for seasoning and add the zucchini, peas, beans, cabbage, and pasta. Simmer until the pasta is al dente.

Meanwhile, to make the pesto, place the garlic, pine nuts, basil, and Parmesan in a food processor and mix to a paste. Alternatively, use a mortar and pestle. Add the oil in a steady stream, mixing continuously. Season to taste. Serve the soup with a dollop of pesto and the Parmesan.

Serves 6

Moroccan lamb, chickpea, and cilantro soup

³/₄ cup dried chickpeas
1 tablespoon olive oil
1³/₄ lb. boneless leg of lamb, cut into
    ½ inch cubes
1 onion, chopped
2 garlic cloves, crushed
½ teaspoon ground cinnamon
½ teaspoon ground turmeric
½ teaspoon ground ginger
4 tablespoons chopped cilantro
2 x 14 oz. cans chopped tomatoes
4 cups chicken stock
²/₃ cup dried red lentils, rinsed
cilantro, to garnish

Soak the chickpeas in cold water overnight. Drain and rinse well.

Heat the oil in a large saucepan over high heat and brown the lamb in batches for 2–3 minutes. Reduce the heat to medium, return the lamb to the saucepan with the onion and garlic, and cook for 5 minutes. Add the spices, season, and cook for 2 minutes. Add the cilantro, tomatoes, stock, and 2 cups water and bring to a boil over high heat.

Add the lentils and chickpeas and simmer, covered, over low heat for 1½ hours. Uncover and cook for 30 minutes or until the lamb is tender and the soup is thick. Season. Garnish with cilantro.

Serves 4–6

Poached seafood broth with soba noodles

9 oz. dried soba noodles
8 jumbo shrimp
1 1/2 tablespoons finely chopped
ginger
4 scallions, cut diagonally
1/3 cup light soy sauce
1/4 cup mirin
1 teaspoon grated palm sugar or light
brown sugar
10 1/2 oz. boneless salmon fillet, skin
removed, cut into 2 inch strips
10 1/2 oz. boneless white fish fillet, skin
removed, cut into 2 inch strips
5 1/2 oz. calamari, cleaned, scored,
and cut into 1 1/4 inch cubes
1 3/4 oz. mizuna lettuce, roughly
chopped (see Note)

Cook the noodles in a large saucepan of boiling water for 5 minutes or until they are tender. Drain and rinse with cold water.

Peel and devein the shrimp, reserving the shells and leaving the tails intact. Place the heads and shells in a large saucepan with the ginger, half the scallions, and 6 cups water. Bring slowly to a boil and boil for 5 minutes. Strain and discard the shrimp heads, shells, and scallions. Return the stock to the saucepan. Add the soy sauce, mirin, and palm sugar to the stock. Heat and stir to dissolve the sugar.

Add the seafood to the saucepan and poach over low heat for 2–3 minutes or until it is just cooked. Add the remaining scallions.

Divide the noodles evenly among four large bowls. Add the seafood, pour the stock on top, and sprinkle with the mizuna lettuce.

Serves 4

Note: Mizuna lettuce has dark green, feathery, glossy leaves and a mild peppery flavor. Young leaves are often used in salads or as a garnish, while older leaves are used in stir-fries or in Japanese cooking.

Red lentil, bulgur, and mint soup

2 tablespoons olive oil
1 large red onion, finely chopped
2 garlic cloves, crushed
2 tablespoons tomato paste
2 tomatoes, finely chopped
2 teaspoons paprika
1 teaspoon cayenne pepper
2 cups red lentils
1/4 cup long-grain rice
8 1/2 cups chicken stock
1/4 cup fine bulgur
2 tablespoons chopped mint
2 tablespoons chopped Italian parsley
1/3 cup plain yogurt
1/4 preserved lemon, pulp removed,
   zest washed and julienned

Heat the oil in a saucepan over medium heat. Add the onion and garlic and cook for 2–3 minutes or until soft. Stir in the tomato paste, tomatoes, and spices and cook for 1 minute.

Add the lentils, rice, and chicken stock, then cover and bring to a boil over high heat. Reduce the heat and simmer for 30–35 minutes or until the rice is cooked.

Stir in the bulgur and herbs, then season to taste. Divide the soup among serving bowls, garnish with yogurt and preserved lemon, and serve immediately.

Serves 4–6

Note: This soup will thicken if allowed to cool, so you may need to add more liquid if you are reheating the soup.

Pork and buttered corn ramen soup

7 oz. Chinese barbecued pork
  (*char sui*) fillet, in one piece
2 small fresh corncobs (1 1/4 lb.)
7 oz. dried ramen noodles
2 teaspoons peanut oil
1 teaspoon grated ginger
6 cups chicken stock
2 tablespoons mirin
2 scallions, sliced diagonally
1 tablespoon unsalted butter
1 scallion, extra, sliced diagonally

Cut the pork into thin slices and remove the corn kernels from the cob using a sharp knife.

Bring a large saucepan of water to a boil, add the ramen noodles, and cook for 4 minutes or until tender. Drain, then rinse in cold water.

Heat the oil in a large saucepan over high heat. Stir-fry the grated ginger for 1 minute. Add the chicken stock and mirin and bring to a boil. Reduce the heat and simmer for 8 minutes.

Add the pork slices to the liquid and cook for 5 minutes, then add the corn kernels and scallions and cook for another 4–5 minutes or until the kernels are tender.

Separate the noodles by running them under hot water, then divide among four deep bowls. Ladle on the soup, then place 1 teaspoon butter on each serving. Garnish with the extra scallion and serve at once.

Serves 4

Note: This soup is traditionally served with the butter on top. However, for a healthier option, it is also quite delicious without the butter.

Oxtail soup with stout and vegetables

4½ lb. oxtails, trimmed
2 tablespoons vegetable oil
2 onions, finely chopped
1 leek, finely chopped
2 carrots, diced
1 celery stalk, diced
2 garlic cloves, crushed
2 bay leaves
2 tablespoons tomato paste
1 thyme sprig
2 sprigs Italian parsley
14 cups chicken stock
1½ cups stout ale
2 tomatoes, seeded and diced
¼ lb. cauliflower florets
¼ lb. green beans
¼ lb. broccoli florets
¼ lb. asparagus spears, cut into
    1¼ inch pieces

Preheat the oven to 400°F. Place the oxtails in a baking dish and bake for 1 hour or until dark golden, turning occasionally. Allow to cool.

Heat the oil in a large saucepan over medium heat and cook the onions, leek, carrots, and celery for 3–4 minutes or until soft. Stir in the garlic, bay leaves, and tomato paste, then add the oxtails, thyme, and parsley.

Add the stock and bring to a boil over high heat. Reduce the heat and simmer for 3 hours or until the oxtails are tender and the meat falls off the bone. Skim off any foam that rises to the surface. Remove the oxtails and cool slightly.

Take the meat off the bones and discard any fat or sinew. Roughly chop and add to the soup with the stout, tomatoes, and 2 cups water. Add the vegetables and simmer for 5 minutes or until the vegetables are tender. Season.

Serves 4

Tomato and red pepper soup with polenta and olive sticks

2 tablespoons vegetable oil
2 tablespoons olive oil
2 red onions, finely chopped
2 garlic cloves, crushed
1 tablespoon ground cumin
1/4 teaspoon ground cayenne pepper
2 teaspoons paprika
2 red bell peppers, diced
1/3 cup tomato paste
1 cup dry white wine
2 x 14 oz. cans diced tomatoes
2 long red chilies, seeded and
  chopped
2 cups chicken or vegetable stock
3 tablespoons chopped Italian parsley
4 tablespoons chopped cilantro

Polenta and olive sticks
2 cups chicken or vegetable stock
1 1/4 cups coarse polenta (cornmeal)
3 1/2 oz. pitted Kalamata olives,
  chopped
1/2 cup olive oil, for deep-frying

Heat the oils in a large saucepan over medium heat and cook the onions and garlic for 2–3 minutes or until soft.

Reduce the heat to low, add the spices, and cook for 1–2 minutes. Add the peppers and cook for 5 minutes. Stir in the tomato paste and wine and simmer for 2 minutes or until reduced slightly. Add the tomatoes, chilies, vegetable stock, and 2 cups water. Season. Simmer for 20 minutes. Purée the soup with the herbs.

To make the polenta and olive sticks, grease a 12 x 8 inch shallow baking pan. Bring the stock and 2 cups water to a boil in a saucepan. Slowly add the polenta in a fine stream, whisking until smooth. Reduce the heat to low. Cook, stirring constantly, for 15–20 minutes or until it starts to come away from the side. Stir in the olives, then spoon into the baking pan, smoothing the surface. Cover and chill for 30 minutes or until firm. Cut into sticks.

Heat the oil in a large, deep frying pan to 375°F or until a cube of bread browns in 10 seconds. Cook the sticks in batches on each side for 1–2 minutes or until crisp. Drain well, then serve with the soup.

Serves 4–6

Chicken and vegetable soup

3¹/₄ lb. chicken
1 onion
2 large leeks, halved lengthwise and
  thoroughly cleaned
3 large celery stalks, halved
5 black peppercorns
1 bay leaf
2 large carrots, peeled and diced
1 large rutabaga, peeled and diced
2 large tomatoes, peeled, seeded,
  and finely chopped
³/₄ cup barley
1 tablespoon tomato paste
2 tablespoons finely chopped Italian
  parsley

Put the chicken, onion, 1 leek, 1 celery stalk, the peppercorns, and bay leaf in a large saucepan and add enough water to cover. Bring to a boil, then reduce the heat and simmer for 1¹/₂ hours, removing any foam that rises to the surface.

Pass the stock through a fine strainer and return to the cleaned saucepan. Discard the onion, leek, celery, peppercorns, and bay leaf and set the chicken aside. When it is cool enough to handle, discard the fat and bones, then shred the flesh, cover, and chill.

Allow the stock to cool, then refrigerate overnight. Skim the fat from the surface, place the stock in a large saucepan, and bring to a boil. Dice the remaining leek and celery and add to the soup with the carrots, rutabaga, tomatoes, barley, and tomato paste. Simmer for 45–50 minutes or until the vegetables are cooked and the barley is tender. Stir in the parsley and shredded chicken. Simmer until warmed through, then season.

Serves 4–6

French onion soup

3½ tablespoons butter
1¾ lb. onions, finely sliced
2 garlic cloves, finely chopped
⅓ cup all-purpose flour
8 cups beef or chicken stock
1 cup white wine
1 bay leaf
2 thyme sprigs
12 slices stale baguette
3½ oz. Gruyère cheese, finely grated

Melt the butter in a heavy-bottomed saucepan and add the onions. Cook over low heat, stirring occasionally, for 25 minutes or until the onions are deep golden brown and beginning to caramelize.

Add the garlic and flour and stir continuously for 2 minutes. Gradually blend in the stock and the wine, stirring all the time, and bring to a boil. Add the bay leaf and thyme and season to taste. Cover the saucepan and simmer for 25 minutes. Remove the bay leaf and thyme and check the seasoning. Preheat the broiler.

Toast the baguette slices, then divide among six warmed soup bowls and ladle the soup over the top. Sprinkle with the grated cheese and broil until the cheese melts and turns light golden brown. Serve immediately.

Serves 6

Pea and ham soup

2¼ cups yellow or green split peas
1½ tablespoons olive oil
2 onions, chopped
1 carrot, diced
3 celery stalks, finely chopped
2¼ lb. ham bones or a smoked ham
  hock, chopped (see Notes)
1 bay leaf
2 thyme sprigs
lemon juice, to taste (optional)

Place the split peas in a large bowl, cover with cold water, and soak for 6 hours. Drain well.

Heat the oil in a large saucepan, add the onions, carrot, and celery, and cook over low heat for 6–7 minutes or until the vegetables are soft but not brown.

Add the peas, ham bones, bay leaf, thyme, and 10 cups cold water and bring to a boil. Reduce the heat and simmer, stirring occasionally, for 2 hours or until the peas are tender, removing any foam that rises to the surface. Remove the bay leaf and thyme and discard them.

Remove the ham bones from the soup, cool slightly, then remove the meat from the bones and discard the bones. Return the ham to the soup and reheat. Season to taste with pepper and lemon juice, if desired.

Serves 6–8

Notes: Ask your butcher to chop the ham bones for you.
For a smoother texture, the soup can be cooled and processed once the ham bones have been removed. Return the meat to the puréed soup.

Watercress soup

2 tablespoons butter
1 onion, finely chopped
1/2 lb. potatoes, diced
2 1/2 cups chicken stock
2 1/4 lb. watercress, trimmed and
  chopped
1/2 cup light whipping cream
1/2 cup milk
freshly grated nutmeg
2 tablespoons chopped chives

Melt the butter in a large saucepan and add the onion. Cover the saucepan and cook over low heat until the onion is softened but not brown. Add the potatoes and chicken stock and simmer for 12 minutes or until the potatoes are tender. Add the watercress and cook for 1 minute.

Remove from the heat and allow the soup to cool a little before pouring into a blender or food processor. Blend until smooth and return to the cleaned saucepan.

Bring the soup gently back to a boil and stir in the cream and milk. Season with nutmeg, salt, and pepper and reheat without boiling. Serve garnished with chives.

Serves 4

Spicy tomato soup with chorizo

1 lb. chorizo sausage
2 tablespoons olive oil
3 onions, halved and sliced
3 garlic cloves, thinly sliced
1/2 teaspoon ground cumin
1 teaspoon paprika
1–2 small red chilies, seeded and
  finely chopped
6 cups chicken stock
14 oz. can diced tomatoes
4 tablespoons chopped Italian parsley

Fill a large, deep frying pan with about 1 1/4 inch cold water. Add the chorizo sausage, then bring to a boil over high heat. Reduce the heat and simmer, turning occasionally, for 15 minutes or until the water evaporates, then continue to cook in any fat left in the pan for 3–4 minutes or until the chorizo is lightly browned. Allow to cool slightly, then break into bite-size pieces.

Heat the oil in a large saucepan over medium heat and cook the onions and garlic for 5–6 minutes or until soft. Stir in the cumin, paprika, chilies, chicken stock, tomatoes, and half the parsley. Bring to a boil, add the chorizo, then reduce the heat and simmer for 20 minutes. Stir in the remaining parsley and serve.

Serves 4–6

South American black bean soup

1 1/2 cups black beans
1 tablespoon vegetable oil
1 onion, finely chopped
1 leek, finely chopped
2 garlic cloves, crushed
2 teaspoons ground cumin
4 slices bacon, diced
4 cups chicken stock
1/3 cup sour cream
1 1/2 tablespoons snipped chives

Soak the black beans in a bowl of cold water overnight. Drain.

Heat the oil in a large saucepan over medium heat and cook the onion, leek, garlic, and cumin for 3 minutes or until soft. Add the bacon and cook for 2–3 minutes or until lightly browned.

Add the black beans, chicken stock, and 2 cups water to the saucepan and bring to a boil over high heat. Reduce the heat and simmer for 1 hour or until the black beans are tender. Season with salt and freshly ground black pepper.

Cool slightly and blend half the soup in batches in a blender until smooth. Return to the saucepan and stir through the unblended soup. Spoon into bowls, add a dollop of sour cream, and garnish with the chives.

Serves 4

Hot and sour lime soup with beef

4 cups beef stock
2 lemongrass stalks, white part only, halved
3 garlic cloves, halved
1 x 1 inch piece ginger, sliced
1 bunch cilantro, leaves and stalks separated, leaves chopped
4 scallions, thinly sliced diagonally
2 strips lime zest, ½ x 1½ inch
2 star anise
3 small red chilies, seeded and finely chopped
1 lb. beef top round, trimmed
2 tablespoons fish sauce
1 tablespoon grated palm sugar or light brown sugar
2 tablespoons lime juice
cilantro leaves, extra, to garnish

Place the stock, lemongrass, garlic, ginger, cilantro stalks, 2 scallions, the lime zest, star anise, 1 teaspoon of the chopped chilies, and 4 cups water in a saucepan. Bring to a boil and simmer, covered, for 25 minutes. Strain and return the liquid to the saucepan.

Heat a ridged grill pan until very hot. Brush lightly with olive oil and sear the steak on both sides until browned on the outside but very rare in the center.

Reheat the soup, adding the fish sauce and palm sugar. Season with salt and black pepper. Add the lime juice to taste (you may want more than 2 tablespoons)—you should achieve a hot and sour flavor.

Add the remaining scallion slices and the chopped cilantro leaves to the soup. Slice the beef across the grain into thin strips. Curl the strips into a decorative pattern, then place in the center of four deep serving bowls. Pour the soup over the beef and garnish with the remaining chili pieces and a few extra cilantro leaves.

Serves 4

Pasta and bean soup

1 cup dried cranberry beans
¼ cup olive oil
3¼ oz. piece pancetta or bacon,
  finely diced
1 onion, finely chopped
2 garlic cloves, crushed
1 celery stalk, thinly sliced
1 carrot, diced
1 bay leaf
1 sprig rosemary
1 sprig Italian parsley
14 oz. can diced tomatoes, drained
6½ cups vegetable stock
2 tablespoons finely chopped Italian
  parsley
5½ oz. ditalini or other small dried
  pasta
extra-virgin olive oil, to drizzle
freshly grated Parmesan cheese,
  to serve

Place the cranberry beans in a large
bowl, cover with cold water, and allow
to soak overnight. Drain and rinse.

Heat the oil in a large saucepan, add
the pancetta, onion, garlic, celery,
and carrot, and cook over medium
heat for 5 minutes or until golden.
Season with black pepper. Add the
bay leaf, rosemary, parsley, tomatoes,
stock, and beans and bring to a boil.
Reduce the heat and simmer for
1½ hours or until the beans are
tender. Add more boiling water if
necessary to maintain the liquid level.

Discard the bay leaf and rosemary
and parsley sprigs. Scoop out 1 cup
of the bean mixture and purée in a
food processor or blender. Return
to the saucepan, season with salt
and ground black pepper, and add
the parsley and pasta. Simmer for
6 minutes or until the pasta is al
dente. Remove from the heat and
set aside for 10 minutes. Serve
drizzled with extra-virgin olive oil
and garnished with Parmesan.

Serves 4

Eight treasure noodle soup

1/4 oz. dried shiitake mushrooms
13 oz. thick fresh egg noodles
5 cups good-quality chicken stock
1/4 cup light soy sauce
2 teaspoons Chinese rice wine
7 oz. boneless, skinless chicken
    breasts, cut diagonally into 1/2 inch
    strips
7 oz. Chinese barbecued pork
    (*char sui*), cut into 1/4 inch slices
1/4 onion, finely chopped
1 carrot, cut diagonally into 1/2 inch
    slices
1/4 lb. snow peas, cut in half
    diagonally
4 scallions, thinly sliced

Place the shiitake mushrooms in a heatproof bowl, cover with boiling water, and soak for 20 minutes or until soft. Drain and squeeze out any excess liquid. Discard the woody stems and thinly slice the caps.

Bring a large saucepan of water to a boil and cook the noodles for 1 minute or until cooked through. Drain, then rinse with cold water. Divide evenly into four deep, warmed bowls.

Meanwhile, bring the chicken stock to a boil in a large saucepan over high heat. Reduce the heat to medium and add the soy sauce and rice wine, stirring to combine. Simmer for 2 minutes. Add the chicken and pork and cook for another 2 minutes or until the chicken is cooked through and the pork is heated. Add the onion, carrot, snow peas, shiitake mushrooms, and half the scallions and cook for another minute or until the carrot slices are tender.

Divide the vegetables and meat among the serving bowls and ladle on the hot broth. Garnish each bowl with the remaining scallion slices.

Serves 4

Winter lamb shank soup

1 tablespoon olive oil
2³/₄ lb. lamb shanks
2 onions, chopped
4 garlic cloves, chopped
1 cup red wine
2 bay leaves
1 tablespoon chopped rosemary
10 cups beef stock
15 oz. can crushed tomatoes
³/₄ cup pearl barley, rinsed and
    drained
1 large carrot, diced
1 potato, diced
1 turnip, diced
1 parsnip, diced
2 tablespoons red currant jelly
    (optional)

Heat the oil in a large saucepan over high heat. Cook the lamb shanks for 2–3 minutes or until brown. Remove.

Add the onions to the saucepan and cook over low heat for 8 minutes or until soft. Add the garlic and cook for 30 seconds, then add the wine and simmer for 5 minutes.

Add the shanks, bay leaves, half the rosemary, and 6 cups of the stock to the saucepan. Season. Bring to a boil over high heat. Reduce the heat and simmer, covered, for 2 hours or until the meat falls off the bone. Remove the shanks and cool slightly.

Take the meat off the bone and roughly chop. Add to the broth with the tomatoes, barley, and the remaining rosemary and stock and simmer for 30 minutes. Add the vegetables and cook for 1 hour or until the barley is tender. Remove the bay leaves, then stir in the red currant jelly.

Serves 4

Hot and sour shrimp soup

2¼ lb. medium shrimp
1 tablespoon vegetable oil
2 tablespoons tom yum paste
2 lemongrass stalks (white part only),
  bruised
4 kaffir lime leaves
3 small red chilies, thinly sliced
⅓ cup fish sauce
⅓ cup lime juice
2 teaspoons grated palm sugar or
  light brown sugar
4 scallions, thinly sliced diagonally
4 tablespoons cilantro

Peel and devein the shrimp, leaving the tails intact. Reserve the shrimp shells and heads. Cover the shrimp and refrigerate.

Heat a wok over high heat, add the oil, and swirl to coat. Cook the shrimp shells and heads over medium heat for 8–10 minutes or until they turn orange.

Add the tom yum paste and ¼ cup water and cook for 1 minute or until fragrant. Add 9 cups water, bring to a boil, then reduce the heat and simmer for 20 minutes. Strain into a large bowl, discarding the shrimp shells and heads. Return the stock to the wok.

Add the shrimp, lemongrass, lime leaves, and chilies and simmer for 4–5 minutes or until the shrimp are cooked. Stir in the fish sauce, lime juice, sugar, scallions, and cilantro. Discard the lemongrass and serve immediately.

Serves 4

Goulash soup with dumplings

3 tablespoons olive oil
2¼ lb. beef chuck or round, cut into
  ½ inch cubes
2 large onions, chopped
3 garlic cloves, crushed
1 green bell pepper, chopped
1½ teaspoons caraway seeds,
  ground
3 tablespoons sweet paprika
¼ teaspoon ground nutmeg
pinch cayenne pepper
½ teaspoon sea salt
14 oz. can diced tomatoes
8 cups chicken stock
¾ lb. potatoes, cut into ¾ inch cubes
1 green bell pepper, julienned
2 tablespoons sour cream

Dumplings
1 egg
3 tablespoons finely grated Parmesan
  cheese
⅔ cup self-rising flour
pinch cayenne pepper

Heat half the oil in a saucepan and brown the cubed beef in batches for 1–2 minutes. Remove and set aside. Heat the remaining oil in the same saucepan over low heat. Add the onions, garlic, and chopped pepper and cook for 5–6 minutes or until softened. Stir in the spices and salt for 1 minute.

Return the beef to the saucepan and stir to coat. Stir in the tomatoes and stock and bring to a boil. Reduce the heat to low and simmer, covered, for 1¼ hours. Add the potatoes and cook for 30 minutes. Stir in the julienned pepper and sour cream. Season.

To make the dumplings, mix together all the ingredients and a pinch of salt with a fork to form a soft dough (add 1–2 tablespoons water if necessary). Turn onto a lightly floured surface and knead for 5 minutes or until smooth. Roll ½ teaspoonfuls of the dough into balls, drop into the simmering soup, and cook for 6 minutes or until cooked. Serve.

Serves 4–6

Butternut squash soup

4½ lb. butternut squash
3 tablespoons butter
2 onions, chopped
½ teaspoon cumin seeds
4 cups chicken stock
1 bay leaf
⅓ cup light whipping cream
pinch nutmeg

Peel the squash and chop into small chunks. Melt the butter in a large saucepan, add the onions, and cook over low heat for 5–7 minutes or until soft. Add the cumin seeds and cook for 1 minute, then add the squash pieces, stock, and bay leaf. Increase the heat to high and bring to a boil, then reduce the heat and simmer for 20 minutes or until the squash is soft. Remove the bay leaf and allow the soup to cool slightly.

Blend the soup in batches until it is smooth. Return to the cleaned pan and stir in the cream and nutmeg. Simmer gently until warmed through and season with salt and freshly ground black pepper before serving.

Serves 4

Cauliflower and almond soup with hot cheese rolls

½ cup blanched almonds
1 tablespoon olive oil
1 large leek (white part only), chopped
2 garlic cloves, crushed
2¼ lb. cauliflower, cut into small
  florets
2 red potatoes (about ¾ lb.), cut into
  ½ inch pieces
7 cups chicken stock

Cheese rolls
4 round bread rolls
3 tablespoons softened butter
4½ oz. cheddar cheese, grated
1¾ oz. Parmesan cheese, grated

Preheat the oven to 350°F. Place the almonds on a cookie sheet and toast for 5 minutes or until golden.

Heat the oil in a large saucepan over medium heat and cook the leek for 2–3 minutes or until softened. Add the garlic and cook for 30 seconds, then add the cauliflower, potatoes, and stock. Bring to a boil, then reduce the heat and simmer for 15 minutes or until the vegetables are very tender. Cool for 5 minutes.

Blend the soup with the almonds in batches in a blender until smooth. Season to taste with salt and pepper. Return to the cleaned pan and stir over medium heat until heated through. Serve with the cheese rolls.

To make the cheese rolls, split the rolls and butter both sides. Combine the grated cheeses and divide evenly among the rolls. Sandwich together and wrap in aluminum foil. Bake in the oven for 15–20 minutes or until the cheese has melted.

Serves 4

Spicy

Lamb korma with saffron rice

4½ lb. boneless leg of lamb,
 trimmed of excess fat, cut into
 1¼ inch cubes
1 onion, chopped
2 teaspoons grated ginger
3 garlic cloves, peeled
2 teaspoons ground cilantro
2 teaspoons ground cumin
1 teaspoon cardamom seeds
large pinch cayenne pepper
2 tablespoons ghee or oil
1 onion, sliced, extra
½ cup plain yogurt
½ cup heavy whipping cream
1 cinnamon stick
½ cup ground almonds
toasted slivered almonds, to garnish
cilantro leaves, to garnish

Saffron rice
1 tablespoon butter
3 bay leaves
2 cups basmati rice, washed and then
 soaked in cold water for 30 minutes,
 then drained
¼ teaspoon saffron threads, soaked
 in 2 tablespoons hot water for
 2 minutes
2 cups boiling vegetable stock

Place the lamb in a large bowl. Put the onion, ginger, garlic, spices, and ½ teaspoon salt in a food processor and process to a smooth paste. Add the spice mixture to the lamb and mix well to coat. Marinate for 1 hour.

Heat the ghee in a large saucepan, add the extra onion, and cook over low heat for 7 minutes until the onion is soft. Add the lamb in batches and cook, stirring constantly, for 8 minutes until the lamb changes color. Return all the lamb to the saucepan and stir in the yogurt, cream, cinnamon stick, and ground almonds. Reduce the heat, cover, and simmer, stirring occasionally, for 50 minutes or until the meat is tender. Add a little water if the mixture becomes too dry. Season.

To make the saffron rice, melt the butter gently in a large, deep frying pan, add the bay leaves and rice, and cook, stirring, for 6 minutes or until all the moisture has evaporated. Add the saffron and soaking liquid to the rice with the stock and 1½ cups boiling water. Season. Bring to a boil, then reduce the heat to low and cook, covered, for 15 minutes or until the rice is cooked. Serve the korma with the rice and garnish with the almonds and cilantro.

Serves 4–6

Chicken with chili jam and cashews

Chili jam
10 dried long red chilies
4 tablespoons peanut oil
1 red bell pepper, chopped
1 head garlic, peeled and roughly
   chopped
1/2 lb. red Asian shallots, chopped
1/2 cup grated palm sugar or light
   brown sugar
2 tablespoons tamarind purée
   (see Note)

1 tablespoon peanut oil
6 scallions, cut into 1 1/4 inch pieces
1 lb. boneless, skinless chicken
   breasts, cut into slices
1/3 cup roasted unsalted cashews
1 tablespoon fish sauce
1/2 cup Thai basil

To make the chili jam, soak the chilies in a bowl of boiling water for 15 minutes. Drain, remove the seeds, and chop. Put in a food processor, then add the oil, pepper, garlic, and shallots and blend until smooth.

Heat a wok over medium heat and add the chili mixture. Cook, stirring occasionally, for 15 minutes. Add the sugar and tamarind and simmer for 10 minutes or until it darkens and reaches a jamlike consistency. Remove from the wok.

Clean and reheat the wok over high heat, add the oil, and swirl to coat. Stir-fry the scallions for 1 minute, then add the chicken and stir-fry for 3–5 minutes or until golden brown and tender. Stir in the cashews, fish sauce, and 4 tablespoons of the chili jam. Stir-fry for another 2 minutes, then stir in the basil and serve.

Serves 4

Note: Use a nonstick or stainless steel wok to cook this recipe because the tamarind purée will react with the metal in a regular wok and taint the dish.

Smoky spiced eggplant

1 1/4 lb. eggplants
1 red onion, chopped
1 garlic clove, chopped
1 inch piece of ginger, chopped
1 green chili, chopped
1/3 cup vegetable oil
1/4 teaspoon chili powder
1/2 teaspoon garam masala
2 teaspoons ground cumin
2 teaspoons ground cilantro
2 teaspoons salt
1/2 teaspoon ground black pepper
2 ripe tomatoes, chopped
3–4 tablespoons cilantro, finely
  chopped

Using a pair of tongs, scorch the eggplants by holding them over a medium gas flame. Alternatively, heat them under a broiler or on an electric griddle. Keep turning them until the skin is blackened on all sides. Set aside until cool, then peel off the charred skin. Roughly chop the flesh. Don't worry if black specks remain on the flesh, as they add to the smoky flavor.

Combine the onion, garlic, ginger, and chili in a blender and process until chopped together but not a paste. Alternatively, chop finely with a knife and mix in a bowl.

Heat the oil in a deep, heavy-bottomed frying pan over medium heat, add the onion mixture, and cook until slightly browned. Add all the spices and the salt and pepper and stir for 1 minute. Add the tomatoes and simmer until the liquid has reduced.

Put the eggplants in the pan and mash them with a wooden spoon, stirring around with the spices. Simmer for 10 minutes or until soft. Stir in the cilantro and season with salt. Serve with bread as a light meal or as a cold relish with a main meal such as an Indian curry.

Serves 4

Stir-fried lamb with mint and chilies

2 tablespoons vegetable oil
1³/₄ lb. boneless lamb steaks, thinly
  sliced (see Note)
4 garlic cloves, finely chopped
1 small red onion, cut into wedges
2 small red chilies, thinly sliced
¹/₃ cup oyster sauce
2¹/₂ tablespoons fish sauce
1¹/₂ teaspoons sugar
¹/₂ cup chopped mint leaves
¹/₄ cup whole mint leaves

Heat a wok over high heat, add
1 tablespoon of the oil, and swirl to
coat. Add the lamb and garlic in
batches and stir-fry for 1–2 minutes
or until the lamb is almost cooked.

Heat the remaining oil in the wok, add
the onion, and stir-fry for 2 minutes or
until the onion is soft.

Return all the lamb to the wok. Stir
in the chili, oyster sauce, fish sauce,
sugar, and the chopped mint leaves
and cook for another 1–2 minutes.

Remove from the heat, fold in the
whole mint leaves, and serve with
rice.

Serves 4

Note: Make sure you slice the lamb
across the grain—this will help keep
the meat from breaking up and
shrinking as it cooks.

Pork vindaloo

2¼ lb. leg of pork, on the bone, trimmed of excess fat
6 cardamom pods
1 teaspoon black peppercorns
4 dried chilies
1 teaspoon cloves
4 inch piece of cinnamon stick, roughly broken
1 teaspoon cumin seeds
½ teaspoon ground turmeric
½ teaspoon coriander seeds
¼ teaspoon fenugreek seeds
4 tablespoons clear vinegar (see Note)
1 tablespoon dark vinegar (see Note)
4 tablespoons vegetable oil
2 onions, finely sliced
10 garlic cloves, finely sliced
2 inch piece of ginger, cut into matchsticks
3 ripe tomatoes, roughly chopped
4 green chilies, chopped
1 teaspoon light brown sugar

Remove the bone from the pork and cut the meat into 1 inch cubes. Reserve the bone.

Split open the cardamom pods and remove the seeds. Finely grind the cardamom seeds and all the other spices in a spice grinder or mortar and pestle. In a large bowl, mix the ground spices together with the vinegars. Add the pork and mix thoroughly to coat well. Cover and marinate in the refrigerator for 3 hours.

Heat the oil in a casserole over low heat and fry the onions until lightly browned. Add the garlic, ginger, tomatoes, and chilies and stir well. Add the pork, increase the heat to high, and fry for 3–5 minutes or until browned. Add 1 cup water and any of the marinade liquid left in the bowl, reduce the heat, and bring slowly back to a boil. Add the brown sugar and the pork bone. Cover tightly and simmer for 1½ hours, stirring occasionally, until the meat is very tender. Discard the bone. Season with salt to taste.

Serves 4

Note: "Vindaloo" is Portuguese for "vinegar and garlic." The clear vinegar is made from coconut, the dark from molasses, but white and balsamic vinegars can be used instead.

Spicy corn puffs

2 corncobs
3 tablespoons chopped cilantro
6 scallions, finely chopped
1 small red chili, seeded and finely
 chopped
1 large egg
2 teaspoons ground cumin
1/2 teaspoon ground cilantro
1 cup all-purpose flour
vegetable oil, for deep-frying
sweet chili sauce, to serve

Cut down the side of the corncob with a sharp knife to release the kernels. Roughly chop the kernels, then place them in a large bowl. Holding the corncobs over the bowl, scrape down the sides of the cobs with a knife to release any juice from the cob into the bowl.

Add the cilantro leaves, scallions, chili, egg, cumin, ground coriander, 1 teaspoon salt, and some cracked black pepper to the bowl and stir well. Add the flour and mix well. The texture of the batter will vary depending on the juiciness of the corn. If the mixture is too dry, add 1 tablespoon water, but no more than that as the batter should be quite dry. Allow to rest for 10 minutes.

Fill a large, heavy-bottomed saucepan or deep-fryer one-third full of oil and heat to 350°F or until a cube of bread dropped in the oil browns in 15 seconds. Drop slightly heaping teaspoons of the corn batter into the oil and cook for 1 1/2 minutes or until puffed and golden. Drain on crumpled paper towels and serve immediately with a bowl of the sweet chili sauce to dip the puffs into.

Makes about 36

Chili plum beef

2 tablespoons vegetable oil
1 1/4 lb. lean beef fillet, thinly sliced
  across the grain
1 large red onion, cut into wedges
1 red bell pepper, thinly sliced
1 1/2 tablespoons chili garlic sauce
1/2 cup good-quality plum sauce
1 tablespoon light soy sauce
2 teaspoons rice vinegar
good pinch of finely ground white
  pepper
4 scallions, sliced diagonally

Heat a wok over high heat, then add
1 tablespoon of the oil and swirl to
coat the side of the wok. Stir-fry the
beef in two batches for 2–3 minutes
per batch or until browned and just
cooked. Remove from the wok.

Heat the remaining oil in the wok, add
the onion, and stir-fry for 1 minute
before adding the pepper and
continuing to stir-fry for 2–3 minutes
or until just tender. Add the chili garlic
sauce and stir for 1 minute, then
return the meat to the wok and add
the plum sauce, soy sauce, rice
vinegar, white pepper, and most of
the scallion slices.

Toss everything together for 1 minute
or until the meat is reheated. Sprinkle
with the remaining scallion slices, then
serve with steamed rice or noodles.

Serves 4

. Singapore pepper crab

Stir-fry sauce
2 tablespoons dark soy sauce
2 tablespoons oyster sauce
1 tablespoon grated palm sugar or
  light brown sugar

4½ lb. blue crabs
1–2 tablespoons peanut oil
⅔ cup butter
2 tablespoons finely chopped garlic
1 tablespoon finely chopped ginger
1 small red chili, seeded and finely
  chopped
1½ tablespoons ground black pepper
1 scallion, green part only, thinly
  sliced diagonally

Mix the ingredients for the sauce in a small bowl and set aside.

Wash the crabs well with a stiff brush. Pull back the apron and remove the top shell from each crab (it should come off easily). Remove the intestine and the gray, feathery gills. Using a large, sharp knife, cut the crab lengthwise through the center of the body to form two halves with the legs attached. Cut each half in half again, crosswise. Crack the thicker part of the legs with the back of a heavy knife or crab crackers.

Heat a wok over high heat, add a little oil, and swirl to coat. Add the crab in a few batches, stir-frying over very high heat for 4 minutes per batch or until the shells turn bright orange, adding more oil if needed. Remove from the wok. Reduce the heat to medium-high, add the butter, garlic, ginger, chili, and pepper, and stir-fry for 30 seconds, then add the stir-fry sauce and simmer for 1 minute or until glossy.

Return the crab to the wok, cover, and stir every minute for 4 minutes or until cooked. Sprinkle with the scallions and serve with rice. Provide bowls of warm water with lemon slices for rinsing sticky fingers.

Serves 4

Spanish crisp potatoes in spicy tomato sauce

olive oil, for deep-frying
2¼ lb. red potatoes, peeled and cut
    into ¾ inch cubes, then rinsed and
    patted completely dry
1 lb. ripe Roma (plum) tomatoes
2 tablespoons olive oil, extra
¼ red onion, finely chopped
2 garlic cloves, crushed
3 teaspoons paprika
¼ teaspoon cayenne pepper
1 bay leaf
1 teaspoon sugar
1 tablespoon chopped Italian parsley

Fill a deep-fryer or large, heavy-bottomed saucepan one-third full of oil and heat to 350°F or until a cube of bread dropped in the oil browns in 15 seconds. Cook the potatoes in batches for 10 minutes or until golden. Drain on crumpled paper towels. Do not discard the oil.

Score a cross in the base of each tomato. Place in a bowl of boiling water for 1 minute, then plunge into cold water and peel the skin away from the cross. Chop the flesh.

Heat the extra olive oil in a saucepan, add the onion, and cook over medium heat for 3 minutes or until soft and golden. Add the garlic, paprika, and cayenne and cook for 1–2 minutes. Add the tomatoes, bay leaf, sugar, and ⅓ cup water and cook, stirring occasionally, for 20 minutes. Cool slightly, remove the bay leaf, then process in a food processor until smooth, adding a little water if needed. Prior to serving, reheat the sauce over low heat. Season well.

Reheat the oil to 350°F. Recook the potato in batches for 2 minutes or until crisp. Drain. Place the potatoes on a platter and pour the sauce over them. Garnish with parsley.

Serves 6

Chili beef

¼ cup kecap manis
2½ teaspoons sambal oelek
2 garlic cloves, crushed
½ teaspoon ground cilantro
1 tablespoon grated palm sugar or
  light brown sugar
1 teaspoon sesame oil
14 oz. fillet of beef, partially frozen,
  thinly sliced
1 tablespoon peanut oil
2 tablespoons chopped roasted
  peanuts
3 tablespoons chopped cilantro

Combine the kecap manis, sambal oelek, garlic, ground cilantro, palm sugar, sesame oil, and 2 tablespoons water in a large bowl. Add the beef slices and coat well. Cover with plastic wrap and refrigerate for 20 minutes.

Heat a wok over high heat, add the peanut oil, and swirl to coat. Add the meat in batches and cook each batch for 2–3 minutes or until browned.

Arrange the beef on a serving platter, sprinkle with the chopped peanuts and cilantro, and serve with steamed rice.

Serves 4

Red curry of roast squash, beans, and basil

1 1/4 lb. squash, peeled and seeded, cut into 1 1/4 inch cubes
2 tablespoons vegetable oil
1 tablespoon store-bought red curry paste
1 2/3 cups coconut cream
1/2 lb. green beans, cut into 1 1/4 inch pieces
2 kaffir lime leaves, crushed
1 tablespoon grated palm sugar or light brown sugar
1 tablespoon fish sauce
1 cup Thai basil leaves, plus extra, to garnish
1 tablespoon lime juice

Preheat the oven to 400°F. Place the squash in a baking dish with 1 tablespoon of the oil and toss to coat. Bake for 20 minutes or until tender.

Heat the remaining oil in a saucepan, add the curry paste, and cook, stirring constantly, breaking up with a fork, over medium heat for 1–2 minutes. Add the coconut cream 1/2 cup at a time, stirring well with a wooden spoon between each addition for a creamy consistency. Add the squash and any roasting juices, the beans, and lime leaves. Reduce the heat to low and cook for 5 minutes.

Stir in the palm sugar, fish sauce, basil, and lime juice. Garnish with extra basil leaves. Serve with rice.

Serves 4

Bombay-style fish

2 garlic cloves, crushed
3 small green chilies, seeded and
  finely chopped
1/2 teaspoon ground turmeric
1/2 teaspoon ground cloves
1/2 teaspoon ground cinnamon
1/2 teaspoon ground cayenne pepper
1 tablespoon tamarind purée
2/3 cup vegetable oil
1 3/4 lb. butterfish or snapper, skinned
1 1/4 cups coconut cream
2 tablespoons chopped cilantro

Mix together the garlic, chilies, spices, tamarind, and 1/2 cup of the oil. Place the fish fillets in a shallow dish and spoon the marinade over them. Turn the fish over, cover, and refrigerate for 30 minutes.

Heat the remaining oil in a large, heavy-bottomed frying pan and add the fish in batches. Cook for 1 minute on each side. Return all the fish to the pan, then reduce the heat to low and add any remaining marinade and the coconut cream. Season with salt and gently cook for 3–5 minutes or until the fish is cooked through and flakes easily. If the sauce is too runny, lift out the fish, simmer the sauce for a few minutes, then pour it over the fish. Garnish with the cilantro.

Serves 4

Kofta in tomato and yogurt sauce

Kofta
1 onion, grated
1 lb. ground lamb
3/4 inch piece of ginger, grated
3 garlic cloves, finely chopped
2 green chilies, seeded and finely chopped
1/2 teaspoon salt
1 egg

Tomato and yogurt sauce
2 teaspoons coriander seeds
2 teaspoons cumin seeds
3 tablespoons vegetable oil
4 inch piece of cinnamon stick
6 cloves
6 cardamom pods
1 onion, finely chopped
1/2 teaspoon ground turmeric
1 teaspoon paprika
1 teaspoon garam masala
1/2 teaspoon salt
7 oz. can diced tomatoes
2/3 cup yogurt

cilantro leaves, to garnish
naan bread, to serve

To make the kofta, put the onion in a strainer and use a spoon to press out as much of the liquid as possible. Put it in a bowl and mix in the lamb, ginger, garlic, chilies, salt, and egg. Divide into twenty equal portions and shape each into a ball. Cover with plastic wrap and refrigerate for 2 hours, or put in the freezer while you make the sauce.

To make the sauce, dry-roast the coriander seeds in a small pan over low heat until aromatic. Remove, then dry-roast the cumin seeds. Grind the roasted spices to a fine powder using a spice grinder or mortar and pestle.

Heat the oil in a heavy-bottomed frying pan over low heat. Add the cinnamon stick, cloves, cardamom pods, and onion and fry until the onion is golden. Add all the ground spices and the salt and fry for 30 seconds. Stir in the tomatoes, then remove from the heat and slowly stir in the yogurt. Return the pan to the heat, slide in the chilled meatballs, and bring to a boil. Simmer, uncovered, for 1 hour over very low heat, shaking the pan from time to time to prevent the meatballs from sticking (add a little water if the sauce dries out). Remove any whole spices before serving. Garnish with cilantro and serve with naan bread.

Serves 4

Easy chicken stir-fry

1 tablespoon cornstarch
2 teaspoons finely chopped ginger
2 garlic cloves, crushed
1 small red chili, finely chopped
1 teaspoon sesame oil
¼ cup light soy sauce
1 lb. chicken breasts, thinly sliced
1 tablespoon peanut oil
1 onion, halved and thinly sliced
¼ lb. baby corn, halved diagonally
1 lb. baby bok choy, trimmed and
    quartered lengthwise
2 tablespoons oyster sauce
¼ cup chicken stock

Combine half the cornstarch with the ginger, crushed garlic, chili, sesame oil, and 2 tablespoons soy sauce in a large bowl. Add the chicken, toss until well coated, and marinate for 10 minutes.

Heat a wok over high heat, add the peanut oil, and swirl to coat. Stir-fry the onion for 2 minutes or until soft and golden. Add the chicken in two batches and stir-fry for 5 minutes or until almost cooked through. Add the baby corn and stir-fry for another 2 minutes, then add the bok choy and cook for 2 minutes or until wilted.

Mix the remaining soy sauce and cornstarch with the oyster sauce and chicken stock in a small bowl, add to the wok, and stir-fry for 1–2 minutes or until the sauce has thickened to coating consistency and the chicken is cooked. Serve immediately with steamed rice or noodles.

Serves 4

Jungle curry shrimp

Curry paste
10–12 large dried red chilies
1 teaspoon white pepper
4 red Asian shallots, chopped
4 garlic cloves, sliced
1 lemongrass stalk, white part only,
    sliced
1 tablespoon finely chopped galangal
2 small cilantro roots, chopped
1 tablespoon finely chopped ginger
1 tablespoon shrimp paste, dry-
    roasted

1 tablespoon peanut oil
1 garlic clove, crushed
1 tablespoon fish sauce
1/4 cup ground macadamias
1 1/4 cups fish stock
1 tablespoon whiskey
3 kaffir lime leaves, torn
1 1/4 lb. shrimp, peeled and deveined,
    with tails intact
1 small carrot, quartered lengthwise
    and thinly sliced diagonally
1/4 lb. yard-long beans, cut into
    3/4 inch pieces
1/4 cup bamboo shoots
Thai basil leaves, to garnish

To make the curry paste, soak the
chilies in boiling water for 15 minutes.
Drain and chop. Place in a food
processor with the white pepper,
shallots, garlic, lemongrass, galangal,
cilantro roots, ginger, shrimp paste,
and 1 teaspoon salt and blend until
smooth—add a little water, if
necessary, to form a paste.

Heat a wok over medium heat, add
the oil, and swirl to coat the side. Add
the garlic and 3 tablespoons of the
curry paste and cook, stirring, for
5 minutes. Add the fish sauce, ground
macadamias, fish stock, whiskey, lime
leaves, shrimp, carrot, beans, and
bamboo shoots. Bring to a boil, then
reduce the heat and simmer for
5 minutes or until the shrimp and
vegetables are cooked.

Garnish with Thai basil and freshly
ground black pepper.

Serves 6

Chili lamb chops

4 garlic cloves, crushed
1 tablespoon grated ginger
1 teaspoon vegetable oil
1 teaspoon sambal oelek
2 teaspoons ground coriander
2 teaspoons ground cumin
2 tablespoons soy sauce
2 teaspoons sesame oil
2 tablespoons sweet chili sauce
2 tablespoons lemon juice
12 lamb chops

Combine the garlic, ginger, oil, sambal oelek, coriander, cumin, soy sauce, sesame oil, sweet chili sauce, and lemon juice in a bowl. Season with salt and cracked black pepper.

Place the chops in a nonmetallic dish and pour the marinade on top, coating all sides. Allow to marinate for 20 minutes.

Cook the chops on a very hot ridged grill pan or barbecue for 3 minutes each side or until cooked to your liking. Serve with steamed rice.

Serves 4

Sweet and sour chickpeas

2$^1/_4$ cups chickpeas
2 tablespoons vegetable oil or ghee
2 large red onions, thinly sliced
$^3/_4$ inch piece of ginger, finely
    chopped
2 teaspoons sugar
2 teaspoons ground coriander
2 teaspoons ground cumin
pinch of chili powder (optional)
1 teaspoon garam masala
3 tablespoons tamarind purée
    (see Note)
4 ripe tomatoes, chopped
4 tablespoons cilantro or mint leaves,
    finely chopped

Soak the chickpeas overnight in 8 cups water. Drain, then put the chickpeas in a large saucepan with 8 cups water. Bring to a boil, spooning off any foam from the surface. Cover and simmer over low heat for 1–1$^1/_2$ hours, until soft. It is important they are soft at this stage, as they won't soften any more once the sauce has been added. Drain.

Heat the oil in a heavy-bottomed frying pan. Fry the onions until soft and brown, then stir in the ginger. Add the chickpeas, sugar, coriander, cumin, chili powder, garam masala, and a pinch of salt. Stir, then add the tamarind and tomatoes and simmer for 2–3 minutes. Add 2 cups water, bring to a boil, and cook until the sauce has thickened. Stir in the cilantro or mint. Serve with Indian bread such as rotis or naan.

Serves 6

Note: Tamarind is a souring agent made from the pods of the tamarind tree. It is sold as a block of pulp (including husks and seeds), as cleaned pulp, or as tamarind purée or concentrate.

Panang beef

Paste
8–10 large dried red chilies
6 red Asian shallots, chopped
6 garlic cloves, chopped
1 teaspoon ground coriander
1 tablespoon ground cumin
1 teaspoon white pepper
2 lemongrass stalks, white part only,
  bruised and sliced
1 tablespoon chopped galangal
6 cilantro roots
2 teaspoons shrimp paste
2 tablespoons roasted peanuts

1 tablespoon peanut oil
1 2/3 cups coconut cream
2 1/4 lb. beef round or blade steak, cut
  into 1/2 inch slices
1 2/3 cups coconut milk
1/3 cup crunchy peanut butter
4 kaffir lime leaves
3 tablespoons lime juice
2 1/2 tablespoons fish sauce
3–4 tablespoons grated palm sugar or
  light brown sugar
1 tablespoon chopped roasted
  peanuts, extra, to garnish
Thai basil, to garnish

To make the paste, soak the chilies in a bowl of boiling water for 15 minutes or until soft. Remove the seeds and chop. Place in a food processor with the shallots, garlic, ground coriander, ground cumin, white pepper, lemongrass, galangal, cilantro roots, shrimp paste, and peanuts and process until smooth—add a little water if the paste is too thick.

Place the peanut oil and the thick coconut cream from the top of the can (reserve the rest) in a saucepan and cook over medium heat for 10 minutes or until the oil separates. Add 6–8 tablespoons of the paste and cook, stirring, for 5–8 minutes or until fragrant.

Add the beef, coconut milk, peanut butter, lime leaves, and the reserved coconut cream. Cook for 8 minutes or until the beef just starts to change color. Reduce the heat and simmer for 1 hour or until the beef is tender.

Stir in the lime juice, fish sauce, and sugar. Serve garnished with the peanuts and Thai basil.

Serves 4–6

Cajun shrimp with salsa

Cajun spice mix
1 tablespoon garlic powder
1 tablespoon onion powder
2 teaspoons dried thyme
2 teaspoons ground white pepper
1 1/2 teaspoons cayenne pepper
1/2 teaspoon dried oregano

Tomato salsa
4 plum tomatoes, seeded and
   chopped
1 cucumber, peeled, seeded, and
   chopped
2 tablespoons finely diced red onion
2 tablespoons chopped cilantro
1 tablespoon chopped Italian parsley
1 garlic clove, crushed
2 tablespoons olive oil
1 tablespoon lime juice

2 3/4 lb. large shrimp
1/3 cup butter, melted
2 cups watercress, washed and
   picked through
4 scallions, chopped
lemon wedges, to serve

Combine all the ingredients for the
Cajun spice mix with 2 teaspoons
cracked black pepper.

To make the tomato salsa, combine
the tomatoes, cucumber, onion,
cilantro, and parsley in a bowl. Mix
the garlic, oil, and lime juice together
and season well. Add to the bowl
and toss together.

Peel and devein the shrimp, leaving
the tails intact. Brush the shrimp with
the butter and sprinkle generously with
the spice mix. Cook under a preheated
broiler, turning once, for 2–3 minutes
each side or until a crust forms and
the shrimp are pink and cooked.

Lay some watercress on serving
plates, then spoon the salsa over the
leaves. Arrange the shrimp on top and
sprinkle with some of the chopped
scallions. Serve with lemon wedges
on the side.

Serves 4 as a main dish or 6 as an
appetizer

Chili con carne

2 teaspoons ground cumin
½ teaspoon ground allspice
1–2 teaspoons chili powder
1 teaspoon paprika
1 tablespoon vegetable oil
1 large onion, finely chopped
2 garlic cloves, crushed
2 small red chilies, seeded and finely
  chopped
1¼ lb. ground beef
14 oz. can whole tomatoes
2 tablespoons tomato paste
15 oz. can red kidney beans, drained
  and rinsed
1 cup beef stock
1 tablespoon chopped oregano
1 teaspoon sugar

Heat a small frying pan over medium heat and dry-fry the cumin, allspice, chili, and paprika for 1 minute or until fragrant. Remove from the pan.

Heat the oil in a large saucepan over medium heat and cook the onion for 2–3 minutes or until soft. Add the garlic and chilies and cook for 1 minute. Add the beef and cook over high heat for 4–5 minutes or until the meat is browned, breaking up any lumps with a fork.

Add the tomatoes, tomato paste, kidney beans, stock, oregano, sugar, and spices. Reduce the heat and simmer, stirring occasionally and gently breaking up the tomatoes, for 1 hour or until reduced and thickened. Season with salt and black pepper. Delicious served with tortillas and guacamole (see page 149).

Serves 4

Thai-style seafood curry with tofu

2 tablespoons soybean or
  vegetable oil
1 1/4 lb. firm white fish (cod, halibut,
  or perch), cut into 3/4 inch cubes
1/2 lb. shrimp, peeled and deveined,
  with tails intact
2 x 14 oz. cans coconut milk
1 tablespoon Thai red curry paste
4 fresh or 8 dried kaffir lime leaves
2 tablespoons fish sauce
2 tablespoons finely chopped
  lemongrass (white part only)
2 garlic cloves, crushed
1 tablespoon finely chopped galangal
1 tablespoon shaved palm sugar or
  light brown sugar
10 oz. silken firm tofu, cut into
  1/2 inch cubes
1/4 cup bamboo shoots, julienned
1 large red chili, finely sliced
2 teaspoons lime juice
scallions, chopped, to garnish
cilantro leaves, chopped, to garnish

Heat the oil in a large frying pan or wok. Sear the fish and shrimp over medium heat for 1 minute on each side. Remove from the pan.

Place 1/4 cup coconut milk and the curry paste in the pan and cook over medium heat for 2 minutes or until fragrant and the oil separates. Add the remaining coconut milk, lime leaves, fish sauce, lemongrass, garlic, galangal, palm sugar, and 1 teaspoon salt. Cook over low heat for 15 minutes.

Add the tofu, bamboo shoots, and chili. Simmer for 3–5 minutes. Return to medium heat, add the seafood and lime juice, and cook for 3 minutes or until the seafood is just cooked. Remove from the heat.

Serve with steamed rice and garnish with the chopped scallions and cilantro.

Serves 4

Potato masala

2 tablespoons vegetable oil
1 teaspoon black mustard seeds
10 curry leaves
1/4 teaspoon ground turmeric
1/2 inch piece of ginger, grated
2 green chilies, finely chopped
2 onions, chopped
1 1/4 lb. waxy potatoes, cut into
   3/4 inch cubes
1 tablespoon tamarind purée

Heat the oil in a heavy-bottomed frying pan, add the mustard seeds, and cover. When the seeds start to pop, add the curry leaves, turmeric, ginger, chilies, and onions and cook, uncovered, until the onions are soft.

Add the potato cubes and 1 cup water to the pan, bring to a boil, cover, and cook until the potatoes are tender and almost breaking up. If there is any liquid left in the pan, let it simmer a little, uncovered, until it evaporates. If the potatoes aren't cooked and there is no liquid left, add a little more and continue to cook. Add the tamarind and season with salt.

Serves 4

Note: This filling is traditionally rolled in *dosas*—large pancakes made with rice flour—and served for breakfast or as a snack in southern India. However, it also makes an excellent side dish.

Madras beef curry

1 tablespoon vegetable oil
2 onions, finely chopped
3 garlic cloves, finely chopped
1 tablespoon grated ginger
4 tablespoons madras curry paste
2¼ lb. chuck steak, trimmed and cut
  into 1¼ inch cubes
¼ cup tomato paste
1 cup beef stock
6 new potatoes, halved
1 cup frozen peas

Preheat the oven to 350°F. Heat the oil in a heavy-bottomed, 12 cup, flameproof casserole. Cook the onions over medium heat for 4–5 minutes. Add the garlic and ginger and cook, stirring, for 5 minutes or until the onions are lightly golden, being careful not to burn them.

Add the curry paste and cook, stirring, for 2 minutes or until fragrant. Increase the heat to high, add the meat, and stir constantly for 2–3 minutes or until the meat is well coated. Add the tomato paste and stock and stir well.

Bake, covered, for 50 minutes, stirring 2–3 times during cooking, and add a little water if necessary. Reduce the oven to 315°F. Add the potatoes and cook for 30 minutes, then add the peas and cook for another 10 minutes or until the potatoes are tender. Serve hot with steamed jasmine rice.

Serves 6

Cauliflower with mustard

2 teaspoons yellow mustard seeds
2 teaspoons black mustard seeds
1 teaspoon ground turmeric
1 teaspoon tamarind purée
2–3 tablespoons mustard oil or
  vegetable oil
2 garlic cloves, finely chopped
½ onion, finely chopped
1¼ lb. cauliflower, broken into small
  florets
3 mild green chilies, seeded and finely
  chopped
2 teaspoons kalonji (nigella) seeds or
  black sesame seeds

Grind the yellow and black mustard seeds together to a fine powder in a spice grinder or mortar and pestle. Mix with the turmeric, tamarind purée, and ½ cup water to form a smooth, liquid paste.

Heat 2 tablespoons of the oil in a large, heavy-bottomed saucepan over medium heat until almost smoking. Reduce the heat to low, add the garlic and onion, and fry until golden. Cook the cauliflower in batches, adding more oil if necessary, and fry until lightly browned, then remove. Add the chilies and fry for 1 minute or until tinged with brown around the edges.

Return all the cauliflower to the saucepan, sprinkle it with the mustard mixture and kalonji, and stir well. Increase the heat to medium and bring to a boil, even though there's not much sauce. Reduce the heat to low, cover, and cook until the cauliflower is nearly tender and the seasoning is dry. Sprinkle a little water on the cauliflower as it cooks to prevent it from sticking to the saucepan. If there is still excess liquid when the cauliflower is cooked, simmer with the lid off until it dries out. Season with salt, then remove from the heat. Serve with rice or Indian bread, or as an accompaniment to a meat dish.

Serves 4

Creamy shrimp curry

1 1/4 lb. large shrimp
1 1/2 tablespoons lemon juice
3 tablespoons vegetable oil
1/2 onion, finely chopped
1/2 teaspoon ground turmeric
2 inch piece of cinnamon stick
4 cloves
7 cardamom pods
5 Indian bay leaves (cassia leaves)
3/4 inch piece of ginger, grated
3 garlic cloves, chopped
1 teaspoon chili powder
2/3 cup coconut milk

Peel and devein the shrimp, leaving the tails intact. Put them in a bowl, add the lemon juice, then toss together and leave for 5 minutes. Rinse the shrimp under running cold water and pat dry with paper towels.

Heat the oil in a heavy-bottomed frying pan and fry the onion until lightly browned. Add the turmeric, cinnamon, cloves, cardamom, bay leaves, ginger, and garlic and fry for 1 minute. Add the chili powder, coconut milk, and salt to taste, and slowly bring to a boil. Reduce the heat and simmer for 2 minutes.

Add the shrimp, return to a boil, then reduce the heat and simmer for 5 minutes or until the shrimp are cooked through and the sauce is thick. (Care should be taken not to overcook the shrimp or they will become rubbery.)

Serves 4

Lamb kofta curry

1 lb. ground lamb
1 onion, finely chopped
1 garlic clove, finely chopped
1 teaspoon grated ginger
1 small chili, finely chopped
1 teaspoon garam masala
1 teaspoon ground coriander
1/2 cup ground almonds
2 tablespoons chopped cilantro,
  to garnish

Sauce
1/2 tablespoon vegetable oil
1 onion, finely chopped
3 tablespoons korma curry paste
14 oz. can diced tomatoes
1/2 cup plain yogurt
1 teaspoon lemon juice

Combine the lamb, onion, garlic, ginger, chili, garam masala, ground cilantro, ground almonds, and 1 teaspoon salt in a bowl. Shape into walnut-size balls with your hands.

Heat a large, nonstick frying pan and cook the koftas in batches until brown on both sides—they don't have to be cooked all the way through.

To make the sauce, heat the oil in a saucepan over low heat. Add the onion and cook for 8 minutes or until soft and golden. Add the curry paste and cook until fragrant. Add the tomatoes and simmer for 5 minutes. Stir in the yogurt, 1 tablespoon at a time, and the lemon juice, stirring until combined.

Place the koftas in the tomato sauce. Cook, covered, over low heat for 20 minutes. Serve over steamed rice and garnish with the cilantro.

Serves 4

Beef nachos

2 tablespoons vegetable oil
1 onion, chopped
2 garlic cloves, crushed
1 tablespoon ground cumin
3 teaspoons ground cilantro
1 teaspoon chili powder
14 oz. lean ground beef
1½ cups tomato pasta sauce
15 oz. can refried beans
8 oz. bag plain tortilla chips
2 cups grated cheddar cheese, at
  room temperature
2/3 cup sour cream
4 scallions, green parts included,
  sliced
cilantro leaves, to garnish

Guacamole
2 large, ripe avocados
½ small onion, grated
1–2 jalapeño or serrano chilies,
  seeded and finely chopped (optional)
1 garlic clove, crushed
1 tomato, peeled, seeded, and diced
1 tablespoon lime juice
2 tablespoons chopped cilantro

Preheat the oven to 350°F. Heat the oil in a large frying pan over medium heat and cook the onion, garlic, cumin, ground coriander, and chili powder for 2–3 minutes. Add the ground beef and cook over high heat for 3–4 minutes or until well browned, breaking up any lumps with a fork. Stir in the pasta sauce and refried beans and simmer for 10 minutes or until the mixture thickens.

Meanwhile, to make the guacamole, cut the avocados in half and remove the pits. Scoop out the flesh, place in a small bowl, and mash roughly with a fork. Add the onion, chilies (if using), crushed garlic, tomato, lime juice, chopped cilantro, and ¼ teaspoon salt and stir until well combined.

Divide the tortilla chips among four flameproof serving plates, arranging them close together, with a slight well in the center. Put in the oven for 10 minutes or until the chips are hot and golden. Remove and sprinkle with the grated cheese (the heat from the chips will melt the cheese). Spoon equal quantities of the beef mixture into the well of each pile of chips. Top with the guacamole and sour cream and sprinkle with the scallion slices. Garnish with the cilantro.

Serves 4

Lamb kefta

2¼ lb. ground lamb
1 onion, finely chopped
2 garlic cloves, finely chopped
2 tablespoons finely chopped Italian
   parsley
2 tablespoons finely chopped cilantro
½ teaspoon cayenne pepper
½ teaspoon ground allspice
½ teaspoon ground ginger
½ teaspoon ground cardamom
1 teaspoon ground cumin
1 teaspoon paprika

Sauce
2 tablespoons olive oil
1 onion, finely chopped
2 garlic cloves, finely chopped
2 teaspoons ground cumin
½ teaspoon ground cinnamon
1 teaspoon paprika
2 x 15 oz. cans diced tomatoes
2 teaspoons harissa (see Note)
4 tablespoons chopped cilantro

Preheat the oven to 350°F. Lightly grease two cookie sheets. Place the lamb, onion, garlic, herbs, and spices in a bowl and mix together well. Season with salt and pepper. Roll tablespoons of the mixture into balls and place on the cookie sheets. Bake for 18–20 minutes or until browned.

Meanwhile, to make the sauce, heat the oil in a large saucepan, add the onion, and cook over medium heat for 5 minutes or until soft. Add the garlic, cumin, cinnamon, and paprika and cook for 1 minute or until fragrant.

Stir in the tomatoes and harissa and bring to a boil. Reduce the heat and simmer for 20 minutes, then add the meatballs and simmer for 10 minutes or until cooked through. Stir in the cilantro, season well, and serve.

Serves 4

Note: Harissa is a spicy paste made mainly from chilies and is popular in North African cooking. Look for harissa in gourmet markets.

Yellow curry with vegetables

Yellow curry paste
8 small dried red chilies
1 teaspoon black peppercorns
2 teaspoons coriander seeds
2 teaspoons cumin seeds
1 teaspoon ground turmeric
1½ tablespoons chopped galangal
5 garlic cloves, chopped
1 teaspoon grated ginger
5 red Asian shallots, chopped
2 lemongrass stalks, white part only,
   chopped
1 teaspoon shrimp paste
1 teaspoon finely chopped lime zest

2 tablespoons peanut oil
2 cups coconut cream
½ cup vegetable stock
¼ lb. yard-long beans, cut into
   1¼ inch pieces
¼ lb. fresh baby corn
1 slender eggplant, cut into
   ½ inch slices
¼ lb. cauliflower, cut into small florets
2 small zucchini, cut into ½ inch
   slices
1 small red bell pepper, cut into
   ½ inch slices
1½ tablespoons fish sauce
1 teaspoon grated palm sugar or
   light brown sugar
1 small red chili, chopped, to garnish
cilantro leaves, to garnish

To make the curry paste, soak the chilies in boiling water for 15 minutes. Drain and chop them. Heat a frying pan, add the peppercorns, coriander seeds, cumin seeds, and turmeric, and dry-fry over medium heat for 3 minutes. Transfer to a mortar and pestle or food processor and pound or grind to a fine powder.

Using the mortar and pestle, pound the ground spices, chilies, galangal, garlic, ginger, shallots, lemongrass, and shrimp paste until smooth. Stir in the lime zest.

Heat a wok over medium heat, add the oil, and swirl to coat the side. Add 2 tablespoons of the curry paste and cook for 1 minute. Add 1 cup of the coconut cream. Cook over medium heat for 10 minutes or until thick and the oil separates.

Add the chicken stock, vegetables, and remaining coconut cream and cook for 5 minutes or until the vegetables are tender but still crisp. Stir in the fish sauce and sugar. Garnish with the chopped chili and cilantro leaves.

Serves 4

Toor dal

1 lb. toor dal (yellow lentils)
5 pieces of kokum, each 2 inches
  long (see Note), or tamarind
2 teaspoons coriander seeds
2 teaspoons cumin seeds
2 tablespoons vegetable oil
2 teaspoons black mustard seeds
10 curry leaves
7 cloves
4 inch piece of cinnamon stick
5 green chilies, finely chopped
1/2 teaspoon ground turmeric
14 oz. can diced tomatoes
1 1/2 tablespoons light brown sugar or
  2 teaspoons molasses
cilantro leaves, to garnish

Soak the lentils in cold water for
2 hours. Rinse the kokum, remove
any pits, and put in a bowl with cold
water for a few minutes to soften.
Drain the lentils and place in a heavy-
bottomed pan with 4 cups water and
the kokum. Bring slowly to a boil, then
simmer for 40 minutes or until the
lentils feel soft when pressed.

Place a small frying pan over low heat
and dry-roast the coriander seeds
until aromatic. Remove and dry-roast
the cumin seeds. Grind the roasted
seeds to a fine powder using a spice
grinder or mortar and pestle.

Heat the oil in a small pan over low
heat. Add the mustard seeds and
allow to pop. Add the curry leaves,
cloves, cinnamon, chili, turmeric,
and the roasted spice mix and cook
for 1 minute. Add the tomatoes and
cook for 2–3 minutes or until the
tomatoes are soft and can be broken
up easily. Add the brown sugar or
molasses, then pour the spicy mixture
into the simmering lentils and cook
for 10 minutes. Season with salt.
Garnish with cilantro leaves.

Serves 8

Note: Kokum is the sticky dried purple
fruit of the gamboge tree. It imparts
an acid, fruity flavor to Indian cuisine.
It is sold in Indian markets.

Steamed whole fish with chili, garlic, and lime

2¼–3¼ lb. whole snapper, cleaned
1 lime, sliced
red chilies, finely chopped, to garnish
cilantro leaves, to garnish
lime wedges, to garnish

Sauce
2 teaspoons tamarind concentrate
5 long red chilies, seeded and
  chopped
6 large garlic cloves, roughly chopped
6 cilantro roots and stems
8 red Asian shallots, chopped
1½ tablespoons vegetable oil
2½ tablespoons lime juice
¾ cup shaved palm sugar or
  light brown sugar
3 tablespoons fish sauce

Rinse the fish and pat dry with paper towels. Cut two diagonal slashes through the thickest part of the fish on both sides to ensure even cooking. Place the lime slices in the fish cavity, cover with plastic wrap, and chill until ready to use.

To make the sauce, combine the tamarind with 3 tablespoons water. Blend the chilies, garlic, cilantro, and shallots in a food processor until finely puréed—add a little water if needed.

Heat the oil in a saucepan. Add the paste and cook over medium heat for 5 minutes or until fragrant. Stir in the tamarind, lime juice, and palm sugar. Reduce the heat and simmer for 10 minutes or until thick. Add the fish sauce.

Place the fish on a sheet of waxed paper in a large bamboo steamer and cover. Place over a wok of simmering water—make sure the bottom doesn't touch the water. Cook for 6 minutes per 2¼ lb. fish or until the flesh flakes easily with a fork when tested.

Pour the sauce over the fish and garnish with the chopped chilies, cilantro, and lime wedges. Serve with rice.

Serves 4–6

Seared scallops with chili bean paste

1 lb. hokkien (egg) noodles
¼ cup peanut oil
20 scallops, roe and beards removed
1 large onion, cut into thin wedges
3 garlic cloves, crushed
1 tablespoon grated ginger
1 tablespoon chili bean paste
¼ lb. choy sum, cut into 2 inch
  pieces
¼ cup chicken stock
2 tablespoons light soy sauce
2 tablespoons kecap manis
½ cup cilantro leaves
1 cup bean sprouts
1 long red chili, seeded and finely
  sliced
1 teaspoon sesame oil
1 tablespoon Chinese rice wine

Place the hokkien noodles in a heatproof bowl, cover with boiling water, and soak for 1 minute, until tender and separated. Drain, rinse under cold water, then drain again.

Heat a wok over high heat, add 2 tablespoons of the peanut oil, and swirl to coat the side of the wok. Add the scallops in batches and sear for 20 seconds each side or until sealed. Remove, then wipe the wok clean. Add the remaining oil and swirl to coat. Stir-fry the onion for 2 minutes or until softened. Add the garlic and ginger and cook for 30 seconds. Stir in the chili bean paste and cook for 1 minute or until fragrant.

Add the choy sum to the wok with the noodles, stock, soy sauce, and kecap manis. Stir-fry for 2–3 minutes or until the choy sum has wilted and the noodles have absorbed most of the liquid. Return the scallops to the wok, add the cilantro, bean sprouts, chili, sesame oil, and rice wine, tossing gently until combined.

Serves 4

Beef satay

1 1/2 lb. rump steak, cut into 1 inch
  cubes
2 small garlic cloves, crushed
3 teaspoons grated ginger
1 tablespoon fish sauce
2 small red chilies, seeded and
  julienned

Satay sauce
1 tablespoon peanut oil
8 red Asian shallots, finely chopped
8 garlic cloves, crushed
4 small red chilies, finely chopped
1 tablespoon finely chopped ginger
1 cup crunchy peanut butter
1 2/3 cups coconut milk
1 tablespoon soy sauce
1/3 cup grated palm sugar or
  light brown sugar
3 tablespoons fish sauce
1 kaffir lime leaf
4 tablespoons lime juice

Combine the steak with the garlic,
ginger, and fish sauce and marinate,
covered, in the refrigerator for at least
3 hours. Soak eight wooden skewers
in cold water for 1 hour.

To make the satay sauce, heat the
peanut oil in a saucepan over medium
heat. Cook the shallots, garlic, chilies,
and ginger, stirring occasionally, for
5 minutes or until the shallots are
golden. Reduce the heat to low and
add the peanut butter, coconut milk,
soy sauce, palm sugar, fish sauce,
lime leaf, and lime juice. Simmer for
10 minutes or until thickened, then
remove the lime leaf.

Thread the beef onto the skewers
and cook on a barbecue or ridged grill
pan over high heat for 6–8 minutes or
until cooked through, turning halfway
through the cooking time. Top with
the satay sauce and garnish with the
julienned chilies. Serve with rice.

Serves 4

Lamb kabobs

5 garlic cloves, roughly chopped
2 inch piece of ginger, roughly
    chopped
3 green chilies, roughly chopped
1 onion, roughly chopped
3 tablespoons plain yogurt
3 tablespoons cilantro leaves
½ teaspoon ground black pepper
1 lb. ground lamb
red onion rings, to garnish
lemon wedges, to serve

Combine the garlic, ginger, chilies, onion, yogurt, and cilantro leaves in a food processor to form a thick, smooth paste. If you don't have a processor, chop the vegetables more finely and use a mortar and pestle. Add the pepper, season with salt, then mix in the ground lamb. If you are using a mortar and pestle, mix the ground lamb with the paste in a bowl.

Divide the meat into sixteen portions, about 2 tablespoons each. Shape each portion into an oval patty, cover, and chill for 20 minutes.

Preheat the broiler. Using four metal skewers, thread four meatballs onto each. Broil for 7 minutes or until brown on top. Turn over and brown the other side. Check that the meatballs are cooked. Serve with onion rings and lemon wedges.

Serves 4

Stir-fried beef with yard-long beans and basil

3 bird's-eye chilies, seeded and finely chopped
3 garlic cloves, crushed
2 tablespoons fish sauce
1 teaspoon grated palm sugar or light brown sugar
2 tablespoons peanut or vegetable oil
1 lb. lean fillet of beef, thinly sliced across the grain
1 1/4 cups yard-long beans, sliced into 1 1/4 inch pieces
1 cup Thai basil
thinly sliced bird's-eye chili, to garnish

Combine the chilies, garlic, fish sauce, palm sugar, and 1 tablespoon of the oil in a large, nonmetallic bowl. Add the beef, toss well, then cover and marinate in the refrigerator for 2 hours.

Heat a wok to hot, add 2 teaspoons of the oil, and swirl to coat. Stir-fry the beef in two batches over high heat for 2 minutes per batch or until just browned. Remove from the wok.

Heat the remaining oil in the wok, then add the yard-long beans and 1/4 cup water and cook over high heat for 3–4 minutes, tossing regularly, until tender. Return the beef to the wok with the basil. Cook for another 1–2 minutes or until warmed through. Garnish with chili slices and serve.

Serves 4

Spicy cellophane noodles with ground pork

7 oz. ground pork
1 teaspoon cornstarch
1½ tablespoons light soy sauce
2 tablespoons Chinese rice wine
1 teaspoon sesame oil
5½ oz. cellophane noodles (mung bean vermicelli)
2 tablespoons vegetable oil
4 scallions, finely chopped
1 garlic clove, crushed
1 tablespoon finely chopped ginger
2 teaspoons chili bean sauce
¾ cup chicken stock
½ teaspoon sugar
2 scallions, green part only, extra, thinly sliced diagonally

Combine the pork, cornstarch, 1 tablespoon of the soy sauce, 1 tablespoon of the rice wine, and ½ teaspoon of the sesame oil in a bowl, using a fork or your fingers. Cover with plastic wrap and marinate for 10–15 minutes.

Meanwhile, place the noodles in a heatproof bowl, cover with boiling water, and soak for 3–4 minutes or until softened. Drain well.

Heat a wok over high heat, add the oil, and swirl to coat. Cook the scallions, garlic, ginger, and chili bean sauce for 10 seconds, then add the pork mixture and cook for 2 minutes, stirring to break up any lumps. Stir in the stock, sugar, ½ teaspoon salt, and the remaining soy sauce, rice wine, and sesame oil.

Add the noodles to the wok and toss to combine. Bring to a boil, then reduce the heat to low and simmer, stirring occasionally, for 7–8 minutes or until the liquid is almost completely absorbed. Garnish with the scallion slices and serve.

Serves 4

Rice & Noodles

Sticky rice pockets

20 dried bamboo leaves
1/2 cup vegetable oil
6 scallions, chopped
1 lb. eggplant, cut into 1/2 inch cubes
1/2 cup drained water chestnuts,
  chopped
1 tablespoon mushroom soy sauce
3 small red chilies, seeded and finely
  chopped
2 teaspoons sugar
3 tablespoons chopped cilantro
4 cups white glutinous rice, washed
  and well drained
2 tablespoons soy sauce

Soak the bamboo leaves in boiling water for 10 minutes or until soft. Drain. Heat half the oil in a wok. Cook the scallions and eggplants over high heat for 4–5 minutes or until golden. Stir in the water chestnuts, soy sauce, chilies, sugar, and cilantro. Cool.

Bring 3 cups water to a simmer. Heat the remaining oil in a saucepan, add the rice, and stir for 2 minutes. Stir in 1/2 cup of the hot water over low heat until it is absorbed. Repeat until all the water has been added (about 20 minutes). Add the soy sauce and season with white pepper.

Fold one end of a bamboo leaf diagonally to form a cone. Hold in one hand and spoon in 2 tablespoons of rice. Make an indent in the rice, add 1 tablespoon of eggplant filling, then top with 1 tablespoon of rice. Fold the other end of the leaf over to enclose the filling. Secure with a toothpick and tie tightly with string. Repeat with the remaining bamboo leaves, rice, and filling. Place in a single layer inside a double bamboo steamer. Cover and put over a wok half-filled with simmering water. Steam for 1 1/2 hours or until the rice is tender, adding more boiling water as needed. Serve hot.

Makes 20

Arancini

2 cups risotto rice (arborio, vialone
   nano, or carnaroli)
1 egg, lightly beaten
1 egg yolk
1/2 cup grated Parmesan cheese
all-purpose flour
2 eggs, lightly beaten
dry bread crumbs, to coat
vegetable oil, for deep-frying

Meat sauce
1 dried porcini mushroom
1 tablespoon olive oil
1 onion, chopped
1/4 lb. ground beef or veal
2 slices prosciutto, finely chopped
2 tablespoons tomato paste
1/3 cup white wine
1/2 teaspoon dried thyme leaves
3 tablespoons finely chopped parsley

Cook the rice in boiling water for 20 minutes or until just soft. Drain, without rinsing, and cool. Put in a large bowl and add the egg, egg yolk, and Parmesan. Stir until the rice sticks together. Cover and set aside.

To make the meat sauce, soak the porcini in hot water for 10 minutes, then squeeze dry and chop finely. Heat the oil in a frying pan. Add the mushroom and onion and cook for 3 minutes or until soft. Add the meat and cook, stirring, until browned. Add the prosciutto, tomato paste, wine, thyme, and pepper to taste. Cook, stirring, for 5 minutes or until all the liquid is absorbed. Stir in the parsley and set aside to cool. With wet hands, form the rice mixture into ten balls. Wet your hands again and gently pull the balls apart. Place 3 teaspoons of the meat sauce in the center of each. Reshape to enclose the filling. Roll in the flour, beaten egg, and bread crumbs and chill for 1 hour.

Fill a deep, heavy-bottomed pan one-third full of oil and heat to 350°F or until a cube of bread browns in 15 seconds. Deep-fry the croquettes, two at a time, for 3–4 minutes or until golden. Drain on paper towels and keep warm while cooking the rest.

Makes 10

Tamarind beef, bean, and hokkien noodle stir-fry

Tamarind sauce
1 tablespoon tamarind purée
1 tablespoon vegetable oil
1 onion, finely diced
2 tablespoons palm sugar or light
   brown sugar
2 tablespoons tamari

1 lb. hokkien (egg) noodles (see Note,
   page 191)
4 beef fillets, about 4 oz. each
2 tablespoons vegetable oil
3 garlic cloves, crushed
1 small chili, seeded and diced
3/4 lb. baby green beans, trimmed
1/4 lb. sugar snap peas, trimmed
1 tablespoon mirin
1/4 cup finely chopped cilantro

To make the tamarind sauce, dilute the tamarind in 1 cup hot water. Heat the oil in a saucepan. Add the onion and cook over medium heat for 6–8 minutes or until soft and golden. Add the palm sugar and stir until dissolved. Add the tamarind liquid and tamari and simmer for 5 minutes or until thick.

Rinse the noodles in a colander with warm water to soften—separate with your hands. Drain.

Season the steaks with salt and freshly ground black pepper. Heat half the oil in a large frying pan. Add the steaks and cook on each side for 3–4 minutes or until cooked to your liking. Remove from the pan and allow to rest in a warm place.

Heat the remaining oil in a wok and cook the garlic and chili over high heat for 30 seconds. Add the beans and peas and cook for 2 minutes. Stir in the mirin and cilantro. Add the noodles and toss through to heat.

Divide the noodles among four plates. Top with the steak and drizzle with the tamarind sauce.

Serves 4

Chicken and pork paella

¼ cup olive oil
1 large red bell pepper, seeded and
   cut into ¼ inch strips
1¼ lb. boneless chicken thighs, cut
   into 1¼ inch cubes
7 oz. chorizo sausage, cut into
   ¾ inch slices
½ lb. mushrooms, thinly sliced
3 garlic cloves, crushed
1 tablespoon lemon zest
1½ lb. tomatoes, roughly chopped
½ lb. green beans, cut into
   1¼ inch pieces
1 tablespoon chopped rosemary
2 tablespoons chopped Italian parsley
¼ teaspoon saffron threads dissolved
   in ¼ cup hot water
2 cups short-grain rice
3 cups hot chicken stock
6 lemon wedges

Heat the oil in a large, deep frying pan or paella pan over medium heat. Add the pepper and cook for 6 minutes or until soft. Remove from the pan.

Add the chicken to the pan and cook for 10 minutes or until brown on all sides. Remove. Add the sausage to the pan and cook for 5 minutes or until golden on all sides. Remove.

Add the mushrooms, garlic, and lemon zest and cook over medium heat for 5 minutes. Stir in the tomatoes and pepper and cook for another 5 minutes or until the tomatoes are soft.

Add the beans, rosemary, parsley, saffron mixture, rice, chicken, and sausage. Stir briefly and then add the stock. Do not stir at this point. Reduce the heat and simmer for 30 minutes. Remove the pan from the heat, cover, and allow to rest for 10 minutes. Serve with lemon wedges.

Serves 6

Note: To encourage a thin crust of crispy rice to form, paellas are not stirred right to the bottom of the pan during cooking. The crust is considered one of the best parts of the paella. For this reason, do not use a nonstick frying pan. Paellas are traditionally served at the table from the pan.

Chiang mai noodles

9 oz. fresh thin egg noodles
2 tablespoons vegetable oil
6 red Asian shallots, finely chopped
3 garlic cloves, crushed
1–2 small red chilies, seeded and
  finely chopped
2–3 tablespoons red curry paste
13 oz. boneless, skinless chicken
  breasts, cut into thin strips
2 tablespoons fish sauce
1 tablespoon grated palm sugar or
  light brown sugar
3 cups coconut milk
1 tablespoon lime juice
1 cup chicken stock
4 scallions, sliced, to garnish
1/3 cup cilantro leaves, to garnish
fried red Asian shallot flakes, to
  garnish
store-bought fried noodles, to garnish
red chili, finely diced, to garnish

Cook the egg noodles in a saucepan of boiling water according to the instructions on the package. Drain, cover, and set aside.

Heat a large wok over high heat, add the oil, and swirl to coat. Add the shallots, garlic, and chilies and stir-fry for 3 minutes. Stir in the curry paste and stir-fry for 2 minutes. Add the chicken and stir-fry for 3 minutes or until it changes color.

Stir in the fish sauce, palm sugar, coconut milk, lime juice, and stock. Reduce the heat and simmer over low heat for 5 minutes—do not boil.

To serve, divide the noodles among four deep serving bowls and spoon in the chicken mixture. Garnish with the scallions, cilantro, shallot flakes, fried noodles, and the diced chili.

Serves 4

Phad Thai

9 oz. dried flat rice stick noodles
1 tablespoon tamarind purée
1 small red chili, chopped
2 garlic cloves, chopped
2 scallions, sliced
1½ tablespoons light brown sugar
2 tablespoons fish sauce
2 tablespoons lime juice
2 tablespoons vegetable oil
2 eggs, beaten
5½ oz. pork fillet, thinly sliced
8 large shrimp, peeled and deveined,
  with tails intact
3½ oz. fried tofu puffs, julienned
1 cup bean sprouts
¼ cup chopped roasted peanuts
3 tablespoons cilantro leaves
1 lime, cut into wedges

Place the noodles in a heatproof bowl, cover with warm water, and soak for 15–20 minutes or until the noodles are al dente. Drain well.

Combine the tamarind purée with 1 tablespoon water. Place the chili, garlic, and scallions in a spice grinder (or use a mortar and pestle) and grind to a smooth paste. Transfer the mixture to a bowl and stir in the tamarind mixture along with the sugar, fish sauce, and lime juice, stirring until the ingredients are combined.

Heat a wok until very hot, add 1 tablespoon of the oil, and swirl to coat the side. Add the egg, swirl to coat, and cook for 1–2 minutes or until set. Remove the egg, roll it up, and cut into thin slices.

Heat the remaining oil in the wok, stir in the chili mixture, and stir-fry for 30 seconds. Add the pork and stir-fry for 2 minutes or until tender. Add the shrimp and stir-fry for another minute or until pink and curled.

Stir in the noodles, egg, tofu puffs, and the bean sprouts and gently toss together until heated through. Serve immediately, topped with the peanuts, cilantro, and lime wedges.

Serves 4–6

Risotto Milanese

3/4 cup dry white vermouth
  or white wine
1 large pinch saffron strands
6 cups chicken stock
1/3 cup butter
2 1/2 oz. beef marrow
1 large onion, finely chopped
1 garlic clove, crushed
2 cups risotto rice (arborio, vialone
  nano, or carnaroli)
5 1/2 oz. Parmesan cheese, grated

Put the vermouth in a bowl, add the saffron, and soak for 10 minutes. Heat the chicken stock in a saucepan and maintain at a low simmer.

Melt the butter and beef marrow in a deep, heavy-bottomed saucepan and gently cook the onion and garlic until softened but not browned. Add the rice and reduce the heat to low. Season, then stir to coat the grains of rice in the butter and marrow.

Add the vermouth and saffron to the rice and increase the heat to medium. Cook, stirring, until all the liquid has been absorbed.

Stir in a ladleful of the stock and cook at a fast simmer, stirring continuously. When the stock has been absorbed, stir in another ladleful. Continue like this for about 20 minutes or until the rice is al dente. Add a little more stock or water if you need to—every risotto will use a different amount.

Stir in 3 1/2 oz. of the Parmesan cheese and sprinkle the rest over the top to serve.

Serves 4

Note: This dish is the classic accompaniment to osso buco but is also perfect as an appetizer.

Soba noodles with miso and baby eggplant

9 oz. soba noodles
3 teaspoons dashi granules
1½ tablespoons yellow miso paste
1½ tablespoons Japanese soy sauce
1½ tablespoons mirin
2 tablespoons vegetable oil
½ teaspoon sesame oil
6 baby eggplants, cut into ½ inch
   slices
2 garlic cloves, crushed
1 tablespoon finely chopped ginger
1 cup cooked peas
2 scallions, thinly sliced diagonally
toasted sesame seeds, to garnish

Cook the noodles in a large saucepan of boiling water for 5 minutes. Drain and rinse under cold water.

Dissolve the dashi granules in 1½ cups boiling water. Stir in the miso paste, soy sauce, and mirin.

Heat half the oils in a large frying pan over high heat. Cook the eggplants in two batches for 4 minutes or until golden on both sides. (Use the remaining oil to cook the second batch of eggplants.)

Stir in the garlic and ginger, then the miso mixture, and bring to a boil. Reduce the heat and simmer for 10 minutes or until slightly thickened and the eggplants are cooked. Add the noodles and peas and cook for 2 minutes or until heated through.

Serve the noodles in shallow bowls and garnish with scallion slices and toasted sesame seeds.

Serves 4

Mongolian stew

9 oz. dried rice vermicelli
1 1/4 lb. lamb fillets, thinly sliced across
the grain
4 scallions, sliced
6 cups light chicken stock
1 1/4 x 2 1/2 inch piece ginger, cut into
6 slices
2 tablespoons Chinese rice wine
10 oz. silken firm tofu, cut into 1/2 inch
cubes
3/4 lb. Chinese broccoli (gai larn), cut
into 1 1/2 inch pieces
1 2/3 cups shredded Chinese cabbage

Sauce
1/3 cup light soy sauce
2 tablespoons Chinese sesame paste
1 tablespoon Chinese rice wine
1 teaspoon chili and garlic paste

Place the vermicelli in a large heatproof bowl, cover with boiling water, and soak for 6–7 minutes. Drain well and divide among six serving bowls. Top with the lamb slices and scallions.

To make the sauce, combine the soy sauce, sesame paste, rice wine, and the chili and garlic paste in a bowl.

Put the stock, ginger, and rice wine in a 10 cup, flameproof pot or large saucepan. Cover and bring to a boil over high heat. Add the tofu, Chinese broccoli, and Chinese cabbage and simmer, uncovered, for 1 minute or until the broccoli has wilted. Divide the tofu, broccoli, and cabbage among the serving bowls, then ladle on the hot stock. Drizzle a little of the sauce on top and serve the rest on the side.

Serves 6

Notes: Make sure the stock is hot enough to cook the thin slices of lamb. This recipe traditionally uses a Chinese steamboat. This is an aluminum pot with a steam spout in the middle, which is placed on a propane burner in the middle of the dining table. You could use a fondue pot instead.

Sweet potato and sage risotto

8 slices prosciutto
5 cups chicken stock
½ cup extra-virgin olive oil
1 red onion, cut into thin wedges
¼ lb. orange sweet potatoes, peeled,
   cut into 1 inch cubes
2 cups risotto rice (arborio, vialone
   nano, or carnaroli)
¾ cup shaved Parmesan cheese
3 tablespoons shredded sage
shaved Parmesan cheese, extra,
   to serve

Place the prosciutto slices under a broiler and broil for 1–2 minutes each side or until crispy.

Heat the chicken stock in a saucepan, cover, and keep at a low simmer.

Heat ¼ cup of the oil in a large saucepan, add the onion, and cook over medium heat for 2–3 minutes or until softened. Add the sweet potato cubes and rice and stir through until well coated in the oil.

Stir in a ladleful of the hot stock and cook over moderate heat, stirring continuously. When the stock has been absorbed, stir in another ladleful. Continue like this for about 20 minutes or until all the stock has been added and the rice is creamy and al dente. (You may not need to use all the stock, or you may need a little extra.)

Stir in the shaved Parmesan and 2 tablespoons of the sage. Season. Spoon into four bowls and drizzle with the remaining oil. Break the prosciutto into pieces and sprinkle over the top with the remaining sage. Top with the extra Parmesan, if desired, and serve.

Serves 4

Lamb with hokkien noodles and sour sauce

1 lb. hokkien (egg) noodles (see Note)
2 tablespoons vegetable oil
13 oz. lamb fillets, thinly sliced against the grain
2½ oz. red Asian shallots, peeled and thinly sliced
3 garlic cloves, crushed
2 teaspoons finely chopped ginger
1 small red chili, seeded and finely chopped
1½ tablespoons red curry paste
¼ lb. snow peas, trimmed and cut in half diagonally
1 small carrot, julienned
½ cup chicken stock
1 tablespoon grated palm sugar or light brown sugar
1 tablespoon lime juice
small, whole basil leaves, to garnish

Put the noodles in a bowl, cover with boiling water, and soak for 1 minute. Drain and set aside.

Heat 1 tablespoon of the oil in a wok and swirl to coat the side. Stir-fry the lamb in batches over high heat for 2–3 minutes or until it just changes color. Set aside.

Add the remaining oil, then the shallots, garlic, ginger, and chili and stir-fry for 1–2 minutes. Stir in the curry paste and cook for 1 minute. Add the snow peas, carrot, and the lamb and combine. Cook over high heat, tossing often, for 1–2 minutes.

Add the stock, palm sugar, and lime juice, toss to combine, and cook for 2–3 minutes. Add the noodles and cook for 1 minute or until heated through. Divide among serving bowls and garnish with the basil.

Serves 4–6

Note: Hokkien noodles are thick, fresh egg noodles that have been cooked and lightly oiled before packaging.

Sukiyaki

Sauce
1/2–1 teaspoon dashi granules
1/3 cup soy sauce
2 tablespoons sake
2 tablespoons mirin
1 tablespoon superfine sugar

10 1/2 oz. shirataki noodles (see Notes)
3 tablespoons butter
5 large scallions, cut diagonally into
  1/2 inch slices
16 fresh shiitake mushrooms
  (6 1/2 oz.), cut into smaller pieces
  if too large
1 lb. 12 oz. rump steak, thinly sliced
  across the grain (wrap the beef
  in plastic wrap and freeze for
  40 minutes before cutting, as this
  will make it easier to slice)
3 1/2 oz. watercress, trimmed
4 eggs (optional)

To make the sauce, dissolve the dashi granules in 1/2 cup water in a bowl. Stir in the soy sauce, sake, mirin, and superfine sugar.

Drain the noodles, place in a large heatproof bowl, cover with boiling water, and soak for 2 minutes. Rinse in cold water and drain well.

Melt the butter in a large frying pan over medium heat. Cook the scallions, mushrooms, and beef in batches, stirring continuously, for 1–2 minutes per batch or until just brown. Return all the meat, scallions, and mushrooms to the pan, then add the sauce and watercress. Cook for 1 minute or until the watercress has wilted—the sauce needs to just cover the ingredients.

To serve, divide the noodles among four serving bowls and spoon the sauce evenly over the top. If desired, crack an egg into each bowl and break up through the soup using chopsticks until it is partially cooked.

Serves 4

Notes: Shirataki noodles are sold in Asian food stores. You can also use dried rice vermicelli—soak in boiling water for 5 minutes before use.

Vegetarian paella

1 cup dried navy beans
1/4 teaspoon saffron threads
2 tablespoons olive oil
1 onion, diced
1 red bell pepper, cut into
    1 1/2 x 1/2 inch strips
5 garlic cloves, crushed
1 1/4 cups paella or arborio rice
1 tablespoon sweet paprika
1/2 teaspoon mixed spices
3 cups vegetable stock
14 oz. can diced tomatoes
1 1/2 tablespoons tomato paste
1/4 lb. fresh or frozen soybeans
1/4 lb. Swiss chard leaves (no stems),
    shredded
14 oz. can artichoke hearts, drained
    and quartered
4 tablespoons chopped cilantro

Put the navy beans in a bowl, cover with cold water, and soak overnight. Drain and rinse well. Place the saffron threads in a small frying pan over medium-low heat. Dry-fry, shaking the pan, for 1 minute or until darkened. Remove from the heat and, when cool, crumble into a small bowl. Add 1/2 cup warm water and allow to soak.

Heat the oil in a large paella or frying pan. Add the onion and pepper and cook over medium-high heat for 4–5 minutes or until the onion is soft. Stir in the garlic and cook for 1 minute. Reduce the heat and add the beans, rice, paprika, mixed spices, and 1/2 teaspoon salt. Stir to coat. Add the saffron water, stock, tomatoes, and tomato paste and bring to a boil. Cover, reduce the heat, and simmer for 20 minutes.

Stir in the soybeans, Swiss chard, and artichoke hearts and cook, covered, for 8 minutes or until all the liquid is absorbed and the rice and beans are tender. Turn off the heat and leave for 5 minutes. Stir in the cilantro just before serving.

Serves 6

Fish stew with ginger and tomatoes

1 tablespoon peanut oil
1 onion, cut into thin wedges
1 small red chili, sliced
3 garlic cloves, finely chopped
3/4 x 3/4 inch piece ginger, julienned
1/2 teaspoon ground turmeric
14 oz. can diced tomatoes
4 cups chicken stock
1 tablespoon tamarind purée
3 oz. dried flat rice stick noodles
1 1/4 lb. snapper fillets, skin removed,
   cut into 1 1/4 inch cubes
cilantro leaves, to garnish

Preheat the oven to 425°F. Heat the oil in a frying pan over medium-high heat and cook the onion for 1–2 minutes or until soft. Add the chili, garlic, and ginger and cook for another 30 seconds. Add the turmeric, tomatoes, chicken stock, and tamarind purée and bring to a boil over high heat. Transfer to a 10 cup, heatproof pot or casserole and cook, covered, in the oven for 40 minutes.

Place the noodles in a large heatproof bowl, cover with warm water, and soak for 15–20 minutes or until al dente. Drain, rinse, and drain again.

Remove the pot from the oven and stir in the noodles. Add the fish cubes, then cover and return to the oven for another 10 minutes or until the fish is cooked through. Serve sprinkled with some cilantro leaves.

Serves 4

Chicken and mushroom risotto

5 cups vegetable or chicken stock
2 tablespoons olive oil
10½ oz. boneless, skinless chicken
   breasts, cut into ½ inch wide strips
½ lb. small button mushrooms,
   halved
pinch nutmeg
2 garlic cloves, crushed
1 tablespoon butter
1 small onion, finely chopped
1¾ cups risotto rice (arborio, vialone
   nano, or carnaroli)
⅔ cup dry white wine
3 tablespoons sour cream
½ cup grated Parmesan cheese
3 tablespoons finely chopped Italian
   parsley

Bring the stock to a boil over high heat, reduce the heat, and keep at a low simmer.

Heat the oil in a large saucepan. Cook the chicken pieces over high heat for 3–4 minutes or until golden brown. Add the mushrooms and cook for 1–2 minutes more or until it starts to brown. Stir in the nutmeg and garlic, season with salt and black pepper, and cook for 30 seconds. Remove from the saucepan.

Melt the butter in the same saucepan and cook the onion over low heat for 5–6 minutes. Add the rice, stir to coat, then stir in the wine. Once the wine is absorbed, stir in a ladleful of the hot stock and cook over moderate heat, stirring continuously. When the stock has been absorbed, stir in another ladleful. Continue like this for about 20 minutes or until all the stock has been added and the rice is creamy and al dente. (You may not need to use all the stock, or you may need a little extra.) Stir in the mushrooms and the chicken with the last of the stock.

Remove the saucepan from the heat and stir in the sour cream, Parmesan, and parsley. Season before serving.

Serves 4

Seafood noodles

6 dried shiitake mushrooms
14 oz. fresh thick egg noodles
1 egg white, lightly beaten
3 teaspoons cornstarch
1 teaspoon crushed Szechuan
   peppercorns
1/2 lb. firm white fish, cut into
   3/4 inch cubes
1/2 lb. shrimp, peeled and deveined,
   with tails intact
3 tablespoons peanut oil
3 scallions, sliced diagonally
2 garlic cloves, crushed
1 tablespoon grated ginger
1 cup bamboo shoots, thinly sliced
2 tablespoons hot chili sauce
1 tablespoon soy sauce
2 tablespoons rice wine
3/4 cup fish stock

Soak the mushrooms in 1/2 cup warm
water for 20 minutes. Drain. Discard
the stems, then thinly slice the caps.

Cook the noodles in a saucepan of
boiling water for 2–3 minutes or until
just tender. Drain.

Blend the egg white, cornstarch, and
half the peppercorns to a smooth
paste. Dip the seafood into the
mixture. Heat 2 tablespoons of the oil
in a wok. Drain the excess batter from
the seafood and stir-fry in batches
over high heat until crisp and golden.
Drain on paper towels.

Clean the wok and heat the remaining
oil. Toss the scallions, garlic, ginger,
bamboo shoots, mushrooms, and
remaining pepper over high heat for
1 minute. Stir in the chili sauce, soy
sauce, rice wine, fish stock, and
noodles. Add the seafood and toss
until heated through.

Serves 4

Pancit Canton

1½ tablespoons peanut oil
1 large onion, finely chopped
2 garlic cloves, finely chopped
¾ x ¾ inch piece ginger, shredded
1 lb. boneless chicken thighs,
    trimmed and cut into ¾ inch pieces
4 cups Chinese cabbage, shredded
1 carrot, julienned
7 oz. Chinese barbecued pork (*char sui*), cut into ¼ inch thick pieces
3 teaspoons Chinese rice wine
2 teaspoons sugar
¼ lb. snow peas, trimmed
1½ cups chicken stock
1 tablespoon light soy sauce
8 oz. pancit Canton (or Chinese e-fu) noodles (see Note)
1 lemon, cut into wedges

Heat a wok over high heat, add the oil, and swirl to coat. Add the onion and cook for 2 minutes, then add the garlic and ginger and cook for 1 minute. Add the chicken and cook for 2–3 minutes or until browned. Stir in the cabbage, carrot, pork, rice wine, and sugar and cook for another 3–4 minutes or until the pork is heated and the vegetables are soft. Add the peas and cook for 1 minute. Remove the mixture from the wok.

Add the chicken stock and soy sauce to the wok and bring to a boil. Add the noodles and cook, stirring, for 3–4 minutes or until soft and almost cooked through.

Return the stir-fry mixture to the wok and toss with the noodles for 1 minute or until combined. Divide among four warmed serving dishes and garnish with lemon wedges.

Serves 4

Note: Pancit Canton noodles are used mostly in the Philippines and China, where they are called "birthday" or "long-life" noodles—their length symbolizes a long life for those who eat them. These round cakes of preboiled, deep-fried noodles are delicate and break easily. They are available in Asian markets.

Lion's head meatballs

6 dried Chinese mushrooms
3 1/2 oz. cellophane noodles (mung
   bean vermicelli)
1 1/4 lb. ground pork
1 egg white
4 garlic cloves, finely chopped
1 tablespoon finely grated ginger
1 tablespoon cornstarch
1 1/2 tablespoons Chinese rice wine
6 scallions, thinly sliced
2 cups good-quality chicken stock
2 tablespoons peanut oil
1/4 cup light soy sauce
1 teaspoon sugar
1 lb. bok choy, cut in half lengthwise
   and leaves separated

Soak the mushrooms in 1 cup boiling water for 20 minutes. Drain. Discard the stems and thinly slice the caps. Put the noodles in a heatproof bowl, cover with boiling water, and soak for 3–4 minutes or until soft. Drain and rinse. Preheat the oven to 425°F.

Place the ground pork, egg white, garlic, ginger, cornstarch, rice wine, two-thirds of the scallions, and a pinch of salt in a food processor. Using the pulse button, process until smooth and well combined. Divide the mixture into eight portions and, using wet hands, shape into large balls.

Put the stock in a large saucepan and bring to a boil over high heat, then remove from the heat and keep warm.

Heat the oil in a wok over high heat. Fry the meatballs in batches for 2 minutes each side or until golden but not cooked through. Drain. Place the meatballs, mushrooms, soy sauce, and sugar in a 10 cup, ovenproof clay pot or casserole and cover with the hot stock. Bake, covered, for 45 minutes. Add the bok choy and noodles and bake, covered, for 10 minutes. Sprinkle with the remaining scallions and serve.

Serves 4

Idiyappam

8 oz. rice sticks or vermicelli
4 tablespoons vegetable oil
1/3 cup cashews
1/2 onion, chopped
3 eggs
1 cup fresh or frozen peas
10 curry leaves
2 carrots, grated
2 leeks, finely shredded
1 red bell pepper, diced
2 tablespoons tomato sauce or
  ketchup
1 tablespoon soy sauce
1 teaspoon salt

Soak the rice sticks in cold water for 30 minutes, then drain and put them in a saucepan of boiling water. Remove from the heat and leave in the saucepan for 3 minutes. Drain and rinse in cold water.

Heat 1 tablespoon of the oil in a frying pan and fry the cashews until golden. Remove, add the onion to the pan, fry until dark golden, then drain on paper towels. Cook the eggs in boiling water for 10 minutes to hard-boil, then cool immediately in cold water. When cold, peel them and cut into wedges. Cook the peas in boiling water until tender.

Heat the remaining oil in a frying pan and briefly fry the curry leaves. Add the carrots, leeks, and pepper and stir for 1 minute. Add the tomato sauce, soy sauce, salt, and rice sticks and mix, stirring constantly to prevent the rice sticks from sticking to the pan. Serve on a platter and garnish with the peas, cashews, fried onion, and egg wedges.

Serves 4

Tofu puffs with mushrooms and round rice noodles

8 dried shiitake mushrooms
1 lb. fresh round rice noodles
12 cups good-quality chicken stock
1 carrot, thinly sliced diagonally
3½ oz. fried tofu puffs, cut in half
1¾ lb. bok choy, trimmed and
    quartered
1–1½ tablespoons mushroom soy
    sauce
6 drops sesame oil
ground white pepper, to season
3½ oz. enoki mushrooms, ends
    trimmed

Place the shiitake mushrooms in a heatproof bowl, cover with boiling water, and soak for 20 minutes. Drain and remove the stems, squeezing out any excess water.

Meanwhile, place the noodles in a heatproof bowl, cover with boiling water, and soak briefly. Using your hands, gently separate the noodles and drain well.

Place the chicken stock in a large saucepan, cover, and slowly heat over low heat.

Add the noodles to the simmering stock along with the carrot, tofu puffs, shiitake mushrooms, and bok choy. Cook for 1–2 minutes or until the carrot and noodles are tender and the bok choy has wilted slightly. Stir in the soy sauce and sesame oil and season to taste with white pepper.

Divide the noodles, vegetables, tofu puffs, and enoki mushrooms among four serving bowls, ladle the broth on top, and serve immediately.

Serves 4

Roast pork, Chinese cabbage, and noodle stew

2½ oz. cellophane noodles (mung bean vermicelli)
½ lb. Chinese cabbage
4 cups chicken stock
1 x 1 inch piece ginger, thinly sliced
12 oz. Chinese roast pork, skin removed and reserved (see Note)
2 scallions, thinly sliced diagonally
2 tablespoons light soy sauce
1 tablespoon Chinese rice wine
½ teaspoon sesame oil

Soak the noodles in boiling water for 3–4 minutes. Drain and rinse, then drain again.

Separate the cabbage leaves and cut the leafy ends from the stems. Cut both the cabbage stems and leaves into ¾–1¼ inch squares.

Place the stock and ginger slices in an 8 cup, flameproof casserole and bring to a boil over high heat. Add the cabbage stems and cook for 2 minutes, then add the cabbage leaves and cook for 1 minute. Reduce the heat to medium, add the noodles, and cook, covered, for 4–5 minutes, stirring occasionally.

Meanwhile, cut the pork into ¾ inch cubes and add the scallions, soy sauce, rice wine, and sesame oil. Stir to combine, then cook, covered, for 3–4 minutes and then serve.

Serves 4

Note: If desired, broil the reserved pork skin for 1 minute or until crispy, then arrange on top of each serving.

Porcini risotto

1 oz. dried porcini mushrooms
4 cups chicken or vegetable stock
1/3 cup butter
1 onion, finely chopped
1/2 lb. mushrooms, sliced
2 garlic cloves, crushed
1 3/4 cups risotto rice (arborio, vialone nano, or carnaroli)
pinch of ground nutmeg
1 tablespoon finely chopped parsley
1/2 cup Parmesan cheese, grated

Put the porcini in a bowl, cover with 2 cups hot water, and allow to soak for 15 minutes. Squeeze them dry, reserving the soaking liquid. If the porcini are large, roughly chop them. Strain the soaking liquid into a saucepan and add enough stock to make up to 4 cups. Heat up and maintain at a low simmer.

Melt the butter in a deep, heavy-bottomed frying pan and gently cook the onion until soft but not browned. Add the mushrooms and porcini and fry for a few minutes. Add the garlic, stir briefly, then add the rice and reduce the heat to low. Season and stir to coat the rice with the butter.

Increase the heat to medium and add a ladleful of the stock. Cook at a fast simmer, stirring constantly. When the stock has been absorbed, stir in another ladleful. Continue like this for about 20 minutes or until the rice is creamy and al dente. Add a little more stock or water if you need to—every risotto will use a different amount.

Stir in the nutmeg, parsley, and half the Parmesan, then serve with the rest of the Parmesan sprinkled over the top.

Serves 4

Lamb stew with rice noodles

2 garlic cloves, crushed
2 teaspoons grated ginger
1 teaspoon five-spice powder
1/4 teaspoon ground white pepper
2 tablespoons Chinese rice wine
1 teaspoon sugar
2 1/4 lb. boneless lamb shoulder, trimmed and cut into 1 1/4 inch pieces
1 oz. whole dried Chinese mushrooms
1 tablespoon peanut oil
1 large onion, cut into wedges
3/4 inch piece ginger, julienned
1 teaspoon Szechuan peppercorns, crushed or ground
2 tablespoons sweet bean paste
1 teaspoon black peppercorns, ground and toasted
2 cups chicken stock
1/4 cup oyster sauce
2 star anise
1/4 cup Chinese rice wine, extra
1/3 cup canned sliced bamboo shoots, drained
1/2 cup canned water chestnuts, drained and sliced
14 oz. fresh rice noodles, cut into 3/4 inch wide strips
1 scallion, sliced diagonally

Combine the garlic, grated ginger, five-spice powder, white pepper, rice wine, sugar, and 1 teaspoon salt in a large bowl. Add the lamb and toss to coat. Cover and marinate for 2 hours.

Meanwhile, soak the mushrooms in boiling water for 20 minutes. Drain. Discard the stems and slice the caps.

Heat a wok to high, add the oil, and swirl to coat. Stir-fry the onion, julienned ginger, and Szechuan peppercorns for 2 minutes. Cook the lamb in three batches, stir-frying for 2–3 minutes per batch or until starting to brown. Stir in the bean paste and ground peppercorns and cook for 3 minutes or until the lamb is brown. Add the stock and transfer to an 8 cup, flameproof pot or casserole. Add the oyster sauce, star anise, and extra rice wine and simmer, covered, over low heat for 1 1/2 hours or until the lamb is tender. Stir in the bamboo shoots and water chestnuts and cook for 20 minutes. Add the mushrooms.

Cover the noodles with boiling water and gently separate. Drain and rinse, then add to the stew, stirring for 1–2 minutes or until heated through. Sprinkle with the scallion slices.

Serves 4

Shabu shabu

10½ oz. beef fillet, trimmed
6 cups chicken stock
2½ x ¾ inch piece ginger, thinly sliced
⅓ cup light soy sauce
2 tablespoons mirin
1 teaspoon sesame oil
7 oz. fresh udon noodles
¼ lb. spinach, stems removed and thinly sliced
¾ lb. Chinese cabbage (leaves only), finely shredded
¼ lb. fresh shiitake mushrooms, stems removed and caps thinly sliced
7 oz. firm tofu, cut into ¾ inch cubes
⅓ cup store-bought ponzu sauce (Japanese dipping sauce) or
  ¼ cup soy sauce combined with 1 tablespoon lemon juice

Wrap the beef fillet in plastic wrap and freeze for 40 minutes or until it begins to harden. Remove and slice as thinly as possible across the grain.

Place the stock, ginger, soy sauce, mirin, and sesame oil in a 10 cup, flameproof casserole over medium heat and simmer for 3 minutes. Add the noodles, gently stir with chopsticks to separate them, and cook for 1–2 minutes. Add the spinach, cabbage, mushrooms, and tofu and simmer for 1 minute or until the leaves have wilted.

Divide the noodles among four serving bowls using tongs, then top with the beef slices, vegetables, and tofu. Ladle the hot stock on top and serve the ponzu sauce on the side.

Serves 4

Note: Traditionally, raw beef slices are arranged on a plate with the tofu, mushrooms, vegetables, and noodles. The stock and seasoning are heated on a portable gas flame at the table. Guests dip the meat and vegetables in the hot stock and eat as they go, dipping into the ponzu sauce. The noodles are added at the end and served with the broth.

Indonesian-style fried noodles

14 oz. fresh flat egg noodles
  (1/4 inch wide)
2 tablespoons peanut oil
4 red Asian shallots, thinly sliced
2 garlic cloves, chopped
1 small red chili, finely diced
7 oz. pork tenderloin, thinly sliced
  across the grain
7 oz. boneless, skinless chicken
  breasts, thinly sliced
7 oz. small shrimp, peeled and
  deveined, with tails intact
2 Chinese cabbage leaves, shredded
2 carrots, cut in half lengthwise and
  thinly sliced
3/4 cup yard-long beans, cut into
  1 1/4 inch pieces
1/4 cup kecap manis
1 tablespoon light soy sauce
2 tomatoes, peeled, seeded, and
  chopped
4 scallions, sliced diagonally
1 tablespoon crisp fried onion flakes
Italian parsley, to garnish

Cook the noodles in a large saucepan of boiling water for 1 minute or until tender. Drain and rinse them under cold water.

Heat a wok over high heat, add the oil, and swirl to coat. Stir-fry the Asian shallots for 30 seconds. Add the garlic, chili, and pork and stir-fry for 2 minutes, then add the chicken and cook another 2 minutes or until the meat is golden and tender.

Add the shrimp and stir-fry for another 2 minutes or until pink and just cooked. Stir in the cabbage, carrots, and beans and cook for 3 minutes, then add the noodles and gently stir-fry for 4 minutes or until heated through, being careful not to break up the noodles. Stir in the kecap manis, soy sauce, chopped tomatoes, and scallions and stir-fry for 1–2 minutes.

Season with salt and freshly ground black pepper. Garnish with the fried onion flakes and parsley.

Serves 4

Note: This dish, called *bahmi goreng* in Indonesia, is traditionally eaten with chopped roasted peanuts and sambal oelek on the side. It is also delicious with satay sauce.

Pilaf with onions and spices

1 cup basmati rice
2 cups chicken stock
6 tablespoons ghee or vegetable oil
5 cardamom pods
2 inch piece of cinnamon stick
6 cloves
8 black peppercorns
4 Indian bay leaves (cassia leaves)
1 onion, finely sliced

Wash the rice in a strainer under cold running water until the water from the rice runs clear. Drain.

Heat the stock to near boiling point in a saucepan.

Meanwhile, heat 2 tablespoons of the ghee over medium heat in a large, heavy-bottomed saucepan. Add the cardamom, cinnamon, cloves, peppercorns, and bay leaves and fry for 1 minute. Reduce the heat to low, add the rice, and stir constantly for 1 minute. Add the heated stock and some salt to the rice and bring rapidly to a boil. Cover and simmer over low heat for 15 minutes. Allow the rice to rest for 10 minutes before uncovering. Lightly fluff up the rice before serving.

Meanwhile, heat the remaining ghee in a frying pan over low heat and fry the onion until soft. Increase the heat and fry until the onion is dark brown. Drain on paper towels, then use as a garnish. Serve with casseroles or Indian curries.

Serves 4

Chicken with ponzu sauce and somen noodles

Ponzu sauce
1 tablespoon lemon juice
1 tablespoon lime juice
1 tablespoon rice vinegar
1 tablespoon tamari
1½ tablespoons mirin
2½ tablespoons Japanese soy sauce
2 inch piece kombu (kelp), wiped with
  a damp cloth
1 tablespoon bonito flakes

2 lb. chicken thighs, trimmed and cut
  in half across the bone
4 inch piece kombu (kelp)
7 oz. dried somen noodles
½ lb. shiitake mushrooms (cut into
  smaller pieces if too large)
1 carrot, thinly sliced
10½ oz. baby spinach leaves

To make the sauce, combine all the ingredients in a nonmetallic bowl. Cover with plastic wrap and refrigerate overnight, then pass through a fine strainer.

Put the chicken and kombu in a saucepan with 3½ cups water. Bring to a simmer over medium heat and cook for 20 minutes or until the chicken is cooked, skimming the foam off the surface. Remove the chicken and strain the broth. Transfer the broth and chicken pieces to a 10 cup, flameproof casserole or Japanese *nabe*. Cover and continue to cook over low heat for 15 minutes.

Meanwhile, cook the noodles in a large saucepan of boiling water for 2 minutes or until tender. Drain and rinse under cold running water.

Add the mushrooms and carrot to the chicken and cook for 5 minutes. Put the noodles on top of the chicken, then top with the spinach. Cover and cook for 2 minutes or until the spinach has just wilted. Stir in 4–6 tablespoons of the ponzu sauce and serve.

Serves 4

Note: Traditionally, this dish would be served in a ceramic *nabe* dish, from which the guests help themselves.

Mee grob

4 Chinese dried mushrooms
vegetable oil, for deep-frying
3½ oz. dried rice vermicelli
3½ oz. fried tofu, cut into matchsticks
4 garlic cloves, crushed
1 onion, chopped
1 boneless, skinless chicken breast,
  thinly sliced
8 green beans, sliced diagonally
6 scallions, thinly sliced diagonally
8 raw shrimp, peeled and deveined,
  with tails intact
⅓ cup bean sprouts
cilantro leaves, to garnish

Sauce
1 tablespoon soy sauce
3 tablespoons white vinegar
5 tablespoons sugar
3 tablespoons fish sauce
1 tablespoon sweet chili sauce

Soak the mushrooms in boiling water for 20 minutes. Drain, discard the stems, and thinly slice.

Fill a wok one-third full of oil and heat to 350°F or until a cube of bread browns in 15 seconds. Cook the vermicelli in small batches for 5 seconds or until puffed and crispy. Drain. Add the tofu to the wok in batches and deep-fry for 1 minute or until crisp. Drain. Carefully remove all but 2 tablespoons of oil.

Reheat the wok until very hot and add the garlic and onion and stir-fry for 1 minute. Add the chicken pieces, mushrooms, beans, and half the scallions. Stir-fry for 2 minutes or until the chicken has almost cooked through. Add the shrimp and stir-fry for another 2 minutes or until they just turn pink.

Combine all the sauce ingredients and add to the wok. Stir-fry for 2 minutes or until the meat and shrimp are tender and the sauce is syrupy.

Remove from the heat and stir in the vermicelli, tofu, and bean sprouts. Garnish with the cilantro and remaining sliced scallions.

Serves 4–6

Steamed shrimp rice noodle rolls

Dipping sauce
2 tablespoons light soy sauce
3 tablespoons rice vinegar

3 dried shiitake mushrooms
12 oz. shrimp, peeled and deveined
4 scallions, chopped
2/3 cup chopped snow peas
2 teaspoons finely chopped ginger
2 garlic cloves, crushed
1/2 cup chopped cilantro leaves
1/2 cup chopped water chestnuts
1 teaspoon sesame oil
1 tablespoon light soy sauce
1 egg white
1 teaspoon cornstarch
10 1/2 oz. fresh rice sheet noodles

To make the dipping sauce, combine the soy sauce and rice vinegar.

Cover the mushrooms with hot water and soak for 15 minutes. Drain, discard the stems, and finely chop the caps.

Mince the shrimp in a food processor. Add the mushrooms, scallions, snow peas, ginger, garlic, cilantro, water chestnuts, sesame oil, soy sauce, and a pinch of salt. Add the egg white and cornstarch and pulse until smooth.

Line a large bamboo steamer with waxed paper and place over a wok of simmering water (make sure the bottom doesn't touch the water). Gently unfold the rice sheet noodle and cut into six 6 inch squares. Divide the filling between the six rice noodle squares and spread it out evenly over each. Roll firmly to form a log. Steam, covered, in a wok for 5 minutes. Cut each roll in half and serve with the sauce.

Makes 12

Risi e bisi

6 cups vegetable or chicken stock
2 teaspoons olive oil
3 tablespoons butter
1 small onion, finely chopped
3 oz. pancetta, cut into small cubes
2 tablespoons chopped parsley
2¹/₂ cups shelled young peas
1 cup risotto rice (arborio, vialone
   nano, or carnaroli)
¹/₂ cup Parmesan cheese, grated

Put the stock in a saucepan, bring to a boil, and then maintain at a low simmer. Heat the oil and half the butter in a large, wide, heavy-bottomed saucepan and cook the onion and pancetta over low heat for 5 minutes until softened. Stir in the parsley and peas and add two ladlefuls of the stock. Simmer for 6–8 minutes.

Add the rice and the remaining stock. Simmer until the rice is al dente and most of the stock has been absorbed. Stir in the remaining butter and the Parmesan, season, and serve.

Serves 4

Teriyaki beef with greens and crispy noodles

1 lb. sirloin steak, cut into thin strips
1/2 cup teriyaki marinade
vegetable oil, for deep-frying
3 1/2 oz. dried rice vermicelli
2 tablespoons peanut oil
1 onion, sliced
3 garlic cloves, crushed
1 red chili, seeded and finely chopped
1/2 lb. carrots, julienned
1 1/4 lb. choy sum, cut into
   1 1/4 inch pieces
1 tablespoon lime juice

Combine the beef and teriyaki marinade in a nonmetallic bowl and marinate for 2 hours.

Fill a wok one-third full of oil and heat to 375°F or until a cube of bread browns in 10 seconds. Separate the vermicelli noodles into small bundles and deep-fry until they sizzle and puff up. Drain well on paper towels. Drain the oil and carefully pour it into a heatproof bowl to cool before discarding.

Heat 1 tablespoon of the peanut oil in the wok. When the oil is nearly smoking, add the beef (reserving the marinade) and cook in batches over high heat for 1–2 minutes. Remove to a plate. Heat the remaining oil. Add the onion and stir-fry for 3–4 minutes. Add the garlic and chili and cook for 30 seconds. Add the carrots and choy sum and stir-fry for 3–4 minutes or until tender.

Return the beef to the wok with the lime juice and reserved marinade and cook over high heat for 3 minutes. Add the noodles, toss well briefly, and serve immediately.

Serves 4

Asparagus risotto

2¼ lb. asparagus
2 cups chicken stock
2 cups vegetable stock
4 tablespoons olive oil
1 small onion, finely chopped
1⅔ cups risotto rice (arborio, vialone nano, or carnaroli)
¾ cup Parmesan cheese, grated
3 tablespoons heavy whipping cream

Wash the asparagus and remove the woody ends (hold each spear at both ends and bend it gently—it will snap at its natural breaking point). Separate the tender spear tips from the stems.

Cook the asparagus stems in boiling water for 8 minutes or until very tender. Drain and place in a blender with the chicken and vegetable stocks. Blend for 1 minute, then put in a saucepan, bring to a boil, and maintain at a low simmer.

Cook the asparagus tips in boiling water for 1 minute, drain, and rinse with iced water.

Heat the oil in a large, wide, heavy-bottomed saucepan. Add the onion and cook until soft but not browned. Stir in the rice, season, and reduce the heat to low. Stir in a ladleful of the stock and cook over moderate heat, stirring continuously. When the stock has been absorbed, stir in another ladleful. Continue like this for about 20 minutes, until all the stock has been added and the rice is al dente. (You may not use all the stock, or you may need a little extra—every risotto will be slightly different.) Add the Parmesan and cream and gently stir in the asparagus tips. Season.

Serves 4

Ma po tofu with noodles

1 lb. silken firm tofu, cut into
  3/4 inch cubes
13 oz. hokkien (egg) noodles (see
  Note, page 191)
2 teaspoons cornstarch
1 tablespoon peanut oil
2 teaspoons finely chopped ginger
2 scallions, finely sliced diagonally
8 oz. ground pork
1 1/2 tablespoons salted Chinese black
  beans, rinsed and roughly chopped
  (see Note)
1 tablespoon chili bean paste
1 tablespoon dark soy sauce
1/2 cup chicken stock
1 tablespoon Chinese rice wine
2 garlic cloves, finely chopped
ground white pepper, to taste
2 scallions, green part only, extra,
  finely sliced diagonally
1/2 teaspoon sesame oil

Place the tofu on paper towels to drain the excess moisture.

Place the noodles in a heatproof bowl, cover with boiling water, and soak for 1 minute or until tender and separated. Drain well, rinse under cold water, and drain again. Divide among four serving bowls. Combine the cornstarch and 1 tablespoon water in a small bowl.

Heat the oil in a wok over high heat. Add the ginger and scallions and cook for 30 seconds, then add the ground pork and stir-fry for 2 minutes or until almost cooked. Add the black beans, chili bean paste, and soy sauce and stir-fry for 1 minute. Stir in the chicken stock, rice wine, and tofu and heat through.

Stir the cornstarch mixture and garlic into the wok and cook for another minute or until thickened. Spoon over the noodles and season with ground white pepper. Garnish with the extra scallion and drizzle with the sesame oil.

Serves 4

Note: Chinese black beans are fermented and heavily salted black soybeans. Rinse before use. They are available in cans and packets from Asian markets.

Eggplant with buckwheat noodles

1/4 oz. dried shiitake mushrooms
12 oz. buckwheat (soba) noodles
2 teaspoons sesame oil
3 tablespoons tahini
1 tablespoon light soy sauce
1 tablespoon dark soy sauce
1 tablespoon honey
2 tablespoons lemon juice
3 tablespoons peanut oil
2 long, thin eggplants, cut into very thin strips
2 carrots, julienned
10 scallions, sliced diagonally
6 fresh shiitake mushrooms, thinly sliced
1 cup roughly chopped cilantro

Soak the dried shiitake mushrooms in 1/2 cup hot water for 10 minutes. Drain, reserving the liquid. Discard the woody stems and finely slice the caps.

Cook the noodles in a saucepan of boiling water for 5 minutes or until tender. Drain. Rinse under cold water, then toss with 1 teaspoon of the sesame oil.

Combine the tahini, light and dark soy sauces, honey, lemon juice, 2 tablespoons of the reserved mushroom liquid, and the remaining teaspoon of sesame oil in a food processor until smooth.

Heat 2 tablespoons of the peanut oil over high heat. Add the eggplants and cook, turning often, for 4–5 minutes or until soft and golden. Drain on paper towels.

Heat the remaining oil. Add the carrots, scallions, and fresh and dried mushrooms. Cook, stirring constantly, for 1–2 minutes or until just softened. Remove from the heat and toss with the noodles, eggplants, and dressing. Garnish with the cilantro.

Serves 4–6

Hearty

Shepherd's pie

¼ cup olive oil
1 large onion, finely chopped
2 garlic cloves, crushed
2 celery stalks, finely chopped
3 carrots, diced
2 bay leaves
1 tablespoon thyme, chopped
2¼ lb. good-quality ground lamb
1½ tablespoons all-purpose flour
½ cup dry red wine
2 tablespoons tomato paste
14 oz. can crushed tomatoes
3¼ lb. baking potatoes (such as
    russet), cut into evenly sized pieces
¼ cup milk
⅓ cup butter
½ teaspoon ground nutmeg

Heat 2 tablespoons of the oil over medium heat in a large, heavy-bottomed saucepan and cook the onion for 3–4 minutes or until softened. Add the garlic, celery, carrots, bay leaves, and thyme and cook for 2–3 minutes. Transfer to a bowl and remove the bay leaves.

Add the remaining oil to the same saucepan, add the ground lamb, and cook over high heat for 5–6 minutes or until it changes color. Mix in the flour, cook for 1 minute, then pour in the red wine and cook for 2–3 minutes. Return the vegetables to the saucepan with the tomato paste and crushed tomato. Reduce the heat, cover, and simmer for 45 minutes, stirring occasionally. Season to taste, then transfer to a shallow, 12 cup, flameproof dish and allow to cool. Preheat the oven to 350°F.

Meanwhile, boil the potatoes in salted water over medium heat for 20–25 minutes or until tender. Drain, then mash with the milk and butter until smooth. Season with nutmeg and black pepper. Spoon over the ground lamb and fluff with a fork. Bake for 30 minutes or until golden and crusty.

Serves 6

Sausage and lentil stew

3 tablespoons olive oil
1³/₄ lb. Italian sausages
1 onion, chopped
3 garlic cloves, thinly sliced
1¹/₂ tablespoons chopped rosemary
2 x 14 oz. cans chopped tomatoes
16 juniper berries, lightly crushed
pinch of grated nutmeg
1 bay leaf
1 dried chili, crushed
³/₄ cup red wine
¹/₂ cup green lentils

Heat the oil in a large saucepan and cook the sausages for 5–10 minutes, until browned. Remove the sausages from the saucepan and reduce the heat. Add the onion and garlic to the saucepan and cook gently until the onion is soft.

Stir in the rosemary and then add the tomatoes and cook gently until reduced to a thick sauce. Add the juniper berries, nutmeg, bay leaf, chili, wine, and 1²/₃ cups water. Bring to a boil, then add the lentils and sausages. Give the stew a good stir, cover the saucepan, and simmer gently for about 40 minutes or until the lentils are soft. Stir a couple of times to prevent the lentils from sticking to the bottom of the saucepan. Add a little more water if the lentils are still not cooked.

Serves 4

Cornish pasties

2½ cups all-purpose flour
½ cup butter, chilled and chopped
5½ oz. beef round, finely chopped
1 small potato, finely chopped
1 small onion, finely chopped
1 small carrot, finely chopped
1–2 teaspoons Worcestershire sauce
2 tablespoons beef stock
1 egg, lightly beaten

Grease a cookie sheet. Place the flour, butter, and a pinch of salt in a food processor and process for 15 seconds or until crumbly. Add 4–5 tablespoons of water and process in short bursts until the mixture comes together (add more water if needed). Turn out onto a floured surface and form into a ball. Cover with plastic wrap and chill for 30 minutes. Preheat the oven to 415°F.

Mix together the steak, potato, onion, carrot, Worcestershire sauce, and stock. Season well.

Divide the dough into six portions and roll out each to ⅛ inch thick. Using a 6½ inch diameter plate as a guide, cut out six circles. Divide the filling evenly and put in the center of each pastry circle.

Brush the edges of each pastry circle with beaten egg and form into a semicircle. Pinch the edges to form a frill and place on the cookie sheet. Brush with the remaining beaten egg and bake for 10 minutes. Lower the heat to 350°F. Bake for another 20–25 minutes or until golden.

Makes 6

Vegetable bake

4 large, unpeeled potatoes, halved
1 1/4 lb. unpeeled orange sweet
  potatoes, halved
1 tablespoon butter
1 tablespoon olive oil
2 large leeks, thinly sliced
3 garlic cloves, crushed
6 zucchini, thinly sliced diagonally
1 1/4 cups light whipping cream
1 cup grated Parmesan cheese
1 tablespoon finely chopped thyme
1 tablespoon chopped Italian parsley
1 cup grated cheddar cheese

Preheat the oven to 350°F and grease a deep, 10 cup, flameproof dish. Boil the potato and sweet potatoes for 10 minutes.

Meanwhile, heat the butter and oil in a frying pan. Add the leeks and cook over low heat for 4–5 minutes or until softened. Add a garlic clove and the zucchini and cook for 3–4 minutes or until the zucchini starts to soften. Combine the cream, Parmesan, herbs, and remaining garlic. Season.

When the potatoes and sweet potatoes are cool, peel off the skins and thinly slice. Layer half the potato slices in the bottom of the dish. Season. Spread with a quarter of the cream mixture, then cover with the zucchini mixture, patting down well. Top with another quarter of the cream mixture. Use all the sweet potato slices to make another layer, then cover with half of the remaining cream mixture. Top with the remaining potato slices, then the last of the cream mixture. Season and top with the cheddar.

Bake for 1 1/4 hours or until the vegetables are cooked. Cover with a domed sheet of aluminum foil toward the end if the top starts over-browning. Allow to rest for 10 minutes before cutting.

Serves 6

Baked beef vermicelli cake

⅓ cup butter
1 onion, chopped
1 lb. ground beef
1 lb. 12 oz. tomato pasta sauce
2 tablespoons tomato paste
9 oz. vermicelli or spaghettini
¼ cup all-purpose flour
1¼ cups milk
1¼ cups grated cheddar cheese

Preheat the oven to 350°F. Grease a deep, 9 inch round springform pan. Melt a tablespoon of the butter in a large, deep frying pan and cook the onion over medium heat for 2–3 minutes or until soft. Add the ground beef, breaking up any lumps with the back of a spoon, and cook for 4–5 minutes or until browned. Stir in the pasta sauce and tomato paste, reduce the heat, and simmer for 20–25 minutes. Season.

Cook the pasta in a large saucepan of boiling, salted water until al dente. Drain and rinse. Meanwhile, melt the remaining butter in a saucepan over low heat. Stir in the flour and cook for 1 minute or until pale and foaming. Remove from the heat and gradually stir in the milk. Return to the heat and stir constantly until the sauce boils and thickens. Reduce the heat and simmer for 2 minutes.

Spread half the pasta over the bottom of the pan, then cover with half the meat sauce. Cover with the remaining pasta, pressing it down. Spoon on the remaining meat sauce and then pour on the white sauce. Sprinkle with cheese and cook for 15 minutes. Allow to rest for 10 minutes before removing from the pan. Cut into wedges.

Serves 4–6

Veal parmigiana

¼ cup olive oil
1 garlic clove, crushed
pinch cayenne pepper
pinch superfine sugar
14 oz. can crushed tomatoes
3 teaspoons chopped oregano
⅓ cup all-purpose flour
2 eggs
⅔ cup dry bread crumbs
4 large veal cutlets, well trimmed
⅔ cup mozzarella cheese, thinly
  sliced
⅓ cup grated Parmesan cheese

Preheat the oven to 375°F. Heat
1 tablespoon of the oil in a small
saucepan over medium heat, add the
garlic, and cook for 30 seconds. Add
the cayenne, sugar, tomatoes, and
half the oregano and cook, stirring
occasionally, for 20 minutes or until
thickened. Season well. Place the
flour in a wide, shallow bowl and
season well. Beat the eggs with
2 tablespoons of water in another
bowl. Mix the bread crumbs with
the remaining oregano, season, and
place in a third bowl.

Pound the cutlets between two sheets
of plastic wrap until flattened to
¼ inch thick, being careful not to tear
the flesh from the bone. Coat in the
seasoned flour, shaking off the excess,
then dip both sides in the egg mixture
and then coat in the bread crumbs.
Heat the remaining oil in a large frying
pan. Add the cutlets in two batches
and brown over medium-high heat for
2 minutes on each side. Transfer to a
shallow baking dish large enough to
fit them side by side.

Spread the sauce over each cutlet.
Cover with the mozzarella and
sprinkle with the Parmesan. Bake for
20 minutes or until the cheeses have
melted and browned. Serve.

Serves 4

Lamb tagine

3¼ lb. leg or shoulder of lamb, cut
   into 1 inch pieces
3 garlic cloves, chopped
⅓ cup olive oil
2 teaspoons ground cumin
1 teaspoon ground ginger
1 teaspoon ground turmeric
1 teaspoon paprika
½ teaspoon ground cinnamon
2 onions, thinly sliced
2⅓ cups beef stock
zest of ¼ preserved lemon, rinsed
   and cut into thin strips
15 oz. can chickpeas, drained
1¼ oz. cracked green olives
3 tablespoons chopped cilantro

Place the lamb in a nonmetallic bowl, add the garlic, 2 tablespoons of oil, the cumin, ginger, turmeric, paprika, cinnamon, ½ teaspoon ground black pepper, and 1 teaspoon salt. Mix well to coat and allow to marinate for 1 hour.

Heat the remaining oil in a large saucepan, add the lamb in batches, and brown the meat over high heat for 2–3 minutes. Remove from the saucepan. Add the onions and cook for 2 minutes, return the meat to the saucepan, and add the beef stock. Reduce the heat and simmer, covered, for 1 hour. Add the lemon zest, chickpeas, and olives and cook, uncovered, for another 30 minutes or until the meat is tender and the sauce has reduced and thickened. Stir in the cilantro. Serve in bowls with couscous.

Serves 6–8

Note: If you prefer, you can bake this lamb in the oven in a covered casserole. Preheat the oven to 375°F and cook the tagine for about 1 hour, adding the lemon, chickpeas, and olives after 40 minutes.

Chicken and corn pies

1 tablespoon olive oil
1 1/2 lb. boneless, skinless chicken
  thighs, trimmed and cut into
  1/2 inch pieces
1 tablespoon grated ginger
3/4 lb. oyster mushrooms, halved
3 corncobs, kernels removed
1/2 cup chicken stock
2 tablespoons kecap manis
2 tablespoons cornstarch
1 cup cilantro leaves, chopped
6 sheets unbaked piecrust
milk, to glaze

Grease six metal pie pans measuring approximately 4 inches on the bottom and 1 inch deep. Heat the oil in a large frying pan over high heat and add the chicken. Cook for 5 minutes or until golden. Add the ginger, mushrooms, and corn kernels and cook for 5–6 minutes or until the chicken is just cooked through. Add the stock and kecap manis.

Mix the cornstarch with 2 tablespoons water in a small bowl, then stir into the pan. Boil for 2 minutes before adding the cilantro. Transfer to a bowl, cool a little, then refrigerate for 2 hours or until cold.

Preheat the oven to 350°F. Using a saucer to guide you, cut a 6 inch circle from each sheet of piecrust and line the six pie pans. Fill the shells with the cooled filling, then cut out another six circles large enough to make the lids. Top the pies with the lids, cut away any extra piecrust, and seal the edges with a fork. Decorate the pies with shapes cut from crust scraps. Prick a few holes in the top of each pie, brush with a little milk, and bake for 35 minutes or until golden.

Makes 6

Ratatouille

4 tomatoes
2 tablespoons olive oil
1 large onion, diced
1 red bell pepper, diced
1 yellow pepper, diced
1 eggplant, diced
2 zucchini, diced
1 teaspoon tomato paste
1/2 teaspoon sugar
1 bay leaf
3 thyme sprigs
2 basil sprigs
1 garlic clove, crushed
1 tablespoon chopped parsley

Score a cross in the top of each tomato, plunge into boiling water for 20 seconds, and then peel the skin away from the cross. Chop roughly.

Heat the oil in a frying pan. Add the onion and cook over low heat for 5 minutes. Add the peppers and cook, stirring, for 4 minutes. Remove from the pan and set aside.

Fry the eggplant until lightly browned all over and then remove from the pan. Fry the zucchini until browned and then return the onion, peppers, and eggplant to the pan. Add the tomato paste, stir well, and cook for 2 minutes. Add the tomatoes, sugar, bay leaf, thyme, and basil. Stir well, cover, and cook for 15 minutes. Remove the bay leaf, thyme, and basil.

Mix together the garlic and parsley and add to the ratatouille at the last minute. Stir and serve.

Serves 4

Welsh lamb pie

1³/₄ lb. boneless shoulder of lamb,
  cut into cubes
³/₄ cup all-purpose flour, seasoned
2 tablespoons olive oil
7 oz. bacon, finely chopped
2 garlic cloves, chopped
4 large leeks, sliced
1 large carrot, chopped
2 large potatoes, cut into ½ inch
  cubes
1¼ cups beef stock
1 bay leaf
2 teaspoons chopped Italian parsley
13 oz. puff pastry
1 egg, lightly beaten

Toss the meat in the seasoned flour
and shake off the excess. Heat the
oil in a large frying pan over medium
heat. Cook the meat in batches for
4–5 minutes or until well browned,
then remove from the pan. Add the
bacon and cook for 3 minutes. Add
the garlic and leeks and cook for
5 minutes or until the leeks are soft.

Put the meat in a large saucepan, add
the leeks and bacon, carrot, potatoes,
stock, and bay leaf and bring to a
boil, then reduce the heat, cover, and
simmer for 30 minutes. Uncover and
simmer for 1 hour or until the meat is
cooked and the liquid has thickened.
Season. Remove the bay leaf, stir in
the parsley, and set aside to cool.

Preheat the oven to 400°F. Divide the
filling among four 1½ cup pie dishes.
Divide the pastry into four and roll each
piece out between two sheets of
waxed paper until large enough to
cover the pie. Remove the top sheet
of paper and invert the pastry over the
filling. Trim the edges and pinch to
seal. Cut two slits in the top to allow
steam to escape. Brush with egg and
bake for 45 minutes or until the pastry
is crisp and golden.

Serves 4–6

Beef and red wine stew

2¼ lb. diced beef
¼ cup all-purpose flour, seasoned
1 tablespoon vegetable oil
5½ oz. bacon, diced
8 scallions, greens trimmed to ¾ inch
½ lb. button mushrooms
2 cups red wine
2 tablespoons tomato paste
2 cups beef stock
bouquet garni (see Note)

Toss the beef in the flour until evenly coated, shaking off any excess. Heat the oil in a large saucepan over high heat. Cook the beef in three batches for about 3 minutes or until well browned all over, adding a little extra oil as needed. Remove from the pan.

Add the bacon and cook for 2 minutes or until browned. Remove with a slotted spoon and add to the beef. Add the scallions and mushrooms and cook for 5 minutes or until the onions are browned. Remove.

Slowly pour the red wine into the saucepan, scraping up any sediment from the bottom with a wooden spoon. Stir in the tomato paste and stock. Add the bouquet garni and return the beef, bacon, and any juices to the pan. Bring to a boil, then reduce the heat and simmer for 45 minutes. Return the scallions and mushrooms to the saucepan. Cook for 1 hour or until the meat is tender and the sauce is glossy. Serve with steamed or mashed new potatoes.

Serves 4

Note: To make a bouquet garni, wrap the green part of a leek around a bay leaf, a sprig of thyme, a sprig of parsley, and celery leaves and tie with string. The combination of herbs can be varied according to taste.

Beef, stout, and potato pie

2 tablespoons olive oil
2³/₄ lb. chuck steak, cut into 1¹/₄ inch cubes, excess fat trimmed
2 onions, sliced
2 slices bacon, roughly chopped
4 garlic cloves, crushed
2 tablespoons all-purpose flour
1³/₄ cups stout ale
1¹/₂ cups beef stock
1¹/₂ tablespoons chopped thyme
2 large potatoes, thinly sliced
olive oil, for brushing

Heat 1 tablespoon of the oil over high heat in a large, heavy-bottomed, flameproof casserole, add the beef in batches, and cook, turning occasionally, for 5 minutes or until the meat is nicely colored. Remove from the dish. Reduce the heat to low, add the remaining oil to the dish, then cook the onions and bacon for 10 minutes, stirring occasionally. Add the garlic and cook for another minute. Return the beef to the casserole.

Sprinkle the flour over the beef, cook for a minute, stirring, then gradually add the stout, stirring constantly. Add the stock, increase the heat to medium-high, and bring to a boil. Stir in the thyme, season, then reduce the heat and simmer for 2 hours or until the beef is tender and the mixture has thickened.

Preheat the oven to 400°F. Lightly grease a 5 cup, flameproof dish and pour in the beef mixture. Arrange potato slices in a single overlapping layer over the top to cover the meat. Brush the top of the potato slices with olive oil and sprinkle with salt. Bake for 30–40 minutes or until the potatoes are golden.

Serves 6

Tuna bake

7 oz. short, curly pasta such as cotelli
  or fusilli
4 eggs, hard-boiled and roughly
  chopped
4 scallions, finely chopped
1 tablespoon chopped dill
1 tablespoon lemon juice
½ cup butter
3 teaspoons madras curry powder
⅓ cup all-purpose flour
1½ cups milk
1½ cups light whipping cream
6 oz. mayonnaise
7½ oz. can tuna, drained
2 cups fresh white bread crumbs
1 garlic clove, crushed
1 tablespoon finely chopped Italian
  parsley
2 tablespoons grated Parmesan
  cheese

Preheat the oven to 350°F. Cook the pasta in a large saucepan of rapidly boiling, salted water until al dente. Drain well. Lightly grease an 8 cup, flameproof dish. Combine the egg, scallions, dill, and lemon juice and season to taste.

Melt ¼ cup of the butter in a saucepan, add the curry powder, and cook for 30 seconds. Stir in the flour and cook for 1 minute or until foaming. Remove from the heat, gradually stir in the milk and cream, then return to low heat and stir constantly until the sauce boils and thickens. Reduce to a simmer for 2 minutes, then stir in the mayonnaise. Combine the sauce, cooked pasta, tuna, and egg mixture and spoon into the prepared dish.

Melt the remaining butter in a frying pan, add the bread crumbs and garlic, and cook, stirring, for 1 minute or until the bread crumbs are golden and coated in butter. Stir in the parsley and grated Parmesan and then sprinkle over the tuna mixture. Bake for 15–20 minutes or until golden and heated through.

Serves 6

Orzo and Greek cheese bake

2 cups orzo (rice-shaped pasta)
¼ oz. butter
6 scallions, chopped
1 lb. spinach, stems removed, rinsed
well and chopped
2 tablespoons all-purpose flour
5 cups milk
9 oz. kefalotyri cheese, grated (see
Note)
9 oz. marinated feta cheese, well
drained
3 tablespoons chopped dill

Preheat the oven to 375°F. Cook the pasta in a large saucepan of boiling, salted water until al dente. Drain well, then return to the saucepan. Heat a tablespoon of the butter in a large saucepan over high heat and cook the scallions for 30 seconds. Add the spinach and stir for 1 minute. Season and stir into the orzo.

Put the remaining butter in the saucepan in which the spinach was cooked. Melt over low heat, then stir in the flour and cook for 1 minute or until pale and foaming. Remove from the heat and gradually stir in the milk. Return to the heat and stir constantly for 5 minutes or until the sauce boils and thickens. Add two-thirds of the kefalotyri and all of the feta and stir for 2 minutes or until melted and well mixed. Remove from the heat and stir in the dill.

Combine the pasta mixture with the cheese sauce, season, and pour into a greased 10 cup, flameproof ceramic dish. Sprinkle the remaining cheese over the top and bake for 15 minutes or until golden.

Serves 6

Note: Kefalotyri is a hard Greek sheep's or goat's milk cheese. Parmesan or pecorino cheese can be substituted.

Braised lamb shanks in rich tomato sauce

2 tablespoons olive oil
1 large red onion, sliced
4 lamb shanks (9 oz. each)
2 garlic cloves, crushed
14 oz. can peeled, diced tomatoes
1/2 cup red wine
2 teaspoons chopped rosemary
1 cup instant polenta (cornmeal)
1/4 oz. butter
1/2 cup grated Parmesan cheese

Preheat the oven to 315°F. Heat the oil in a 16 cup, flameproof casserole over medium heat and cook the onion for 3–4 minutes or until soft and translucent. Add the lamb shanks and cook for 2–3 minutes or until lightly browned. Add the garlic, tomatoes, and wine, then bring to a boil and cook for 3–4 minutes. Stir in the rosemary. Season with 1/4 teaspoon each of salt and pepper.

Cover, transfer to the oven, and cook for 2 hours. Remove the lid, return to the oven, and simmer for another 15 minutes or until the lamb just starts to fall off the bone. Check periodically that the sauce is not too dry, adding water if needed.

About 20 minutes before serving, bring 4 cups water to a boil in a saucepan. Add the polenta in a thin stream, whisking continuously, then reduce the heat to very low. Simmer for 8–10 minutes or until thick and coming away from the side of the saucepan. Stir in the butter and Parmesan. To serve, spoon the polenta onto serving plates, top with the shanks, and pour a little sauce from the casserole over the shanks.

Serves 4

Shellfish stew

16 mussels
12 large shrimp, peeled and deveined
1¾ cups cider or dry white wine
¼ cup butter
1 garlic clove, crushed
2 shallots, finely chopped
2 celery stalks, finely chopped
1 large leek, white part only, thinly
  sliced
½ lb. small chestnut mushrooms,
  sliced
1 bay leaf
10 oz. salmon fillet, skinned and cut
  into chunks
14 oz. sole fillet, skin removed, cut
  into thick strips widthwise
1¼ cups heavy whipping cream
3 tablespoons finely chopped parsley

Scrub the mussels and remove their beards. Throw away any that are open and don't close when tapped on the countertop.

Pour the cider into a large saucepan and bring to a simmer. Add the mussels, cover the saucepan, and cook for 3–5 minutes, shaking the saucepan every now and then. Place a fine strainer over a bowl, strain the mussels, then transfer them to a plate, throwing away any that haven't opened. Strain the cooking liquid again through the strainer.

Add the butter to the cleaned saucepan and melt over moderate heat. Add the garlic, shallots, celery, and leek and cook for 7–10 minutes or until the vegetables are just soft. Add the mushrooms and cook for another 4–5 minutes until softened. While the vegetables are cooking, remove the mussels from their shells.

Add the strained liquid to the vegetables in the saucepan, add the bay leaf, and bring to a simmer. Add the salmon, sole, and shrimp and cook for 3–4 minutes, until the fish is opaque and the shrimp are pink. Stir in the cream and cooked mussels and simmer for 2 minutes. Season and stir in the parsley.

Serves 6

Moussaka

2 large eggplants (about 1³/₄ lb.), sliced lengthwise into ½ inch thick pieces
1 tablespoon olive oil
1 large onion, chopped
1 garlic clove, crushed
1 lb. ground beef
½ cup red wine
½ cup tomato paste
pinch of ground cinnamon
2 teaspoons chopped oregano
3 tablespoons chopped Italian parsley
2 tablespoons grated Parmesan cheese
2 tablespoons dry bread crumbs

Sauce
1 tablespoon butter
⅓ cup all-purpose flour
2 cups milk
pinch of ground nutmeg
1 tablespoon grated Parmesan cheese

Preheat the oven to 400°F. Spread the eggplant slices on two foil-lined cookie sheets and brush both sides using a little of the oil. Bake for 10 minutes, turn the slices, and bake for 10 minutes more. Cool.

Heat the remaining oil in a large saucepan. Add the onion and garlic and cook for 4–5 minutes. Increase the heat to high and brown the ground beef for 5 minutes. Stir in the wine, tomato paste, cinnamon, oregano, and a quarter of the parsley. Season. Reduce to a simmer, stirring occasionally, for 15–20 minutes. Remove from the heat.

To make the sauce, melt the butter in a small saucepan. Stir in the flour and cook over low heat for 2–3 minutes. Slowly whisk in the milk, cooking for 6–8 minutes until thickened. Remove from the heat and add the nutmeg, Parmesan, and ½ teaspoon salt.

Grease an 11 x 7 inch casserole. Line the bottom with a layer of eggplant, then top with the ground beef. Cover with the remaining eggplant, then pour the sauce on top. Mix together the Parmesan, bread crumbs, and remaining parsley, then season and sprinkle over the top. Bake for 30 minutes or until golden.

Serves 4–6

Steak and kidney pie

½ cup all-purpose flour, seasoned
3¼ lb. chuck steak, cut into ¾ inch
  cubes
1 lb. ox or beef kidney, cut into
  ¾ inch cubes
2 tablespoons olive oil
2 onions, chopped
¼ lb. button mushrooms, quartered
2 tablespoons butter
1 cup beef or veal stock
¾ cup stout ale
2 tablespoons Worcestershire sauce
1 tablespoon anchovy extract
1 tablespoon chopped Italian parsley
1¼ lb. puff pastry
1 egg, lightly beaten

Place the flour in a bowl. Toss the steak and kidney pieces through the flour and shake off any excess. Heat the oil in a large saucepan over medium heat, add the onions, and cook for 5 minutes. Add the mushrooms and cook for 5 minutes. Remove from the saucepan.

Melt a third of the butter in the saucepan, add a third of the beef and kidney, and cook over medium heat, turning occasionally, for 5 minutes or until brown. Remove and repeat twice with the remaining butter, beef, and kidney. Return all the meat to the saucepan, add the stock and stout, stir, and bring slowly to a boil. Reduce the heat and simmer for 2 hours. Remove from the heat, allow to cool, then add the onion and mushrooms, Worcestershire sauce, anchovy extract, and parsley.

Preheat the oven to 350°F. Place the filling in a ceramic pie dish measuring 8 inches on the bottom and 1½ inches deep. Roll out the pastry between two sheets of waxed paper to fit the top of the pie dish. Moisten the rim of the dish with milk and place the pastry over the filling. Press firmly into place and brush with egg. Decorate with pastry scraps, brush with egg, and bake for 40–45 minutes until golden.

Serves 6

Rich macaroni and cheese

1 lb. elbow macaroni
3 tablespoons butter
1 1/4 cups light whipping cream
1 cup fontina cheese, sliced
4 1/2 oz. provolone cheese, grated
3/4 cup Gruyère cheese, grated
4 1/2 oz. blue castello cheese, crumbled
1/2 cup fresh white bread crumbs
1/4 cup grated Parmesan cheese

Preheat the oven to 350°F. Cook the pasta in a large saucepan of boiling, salted water until al dente. Drain and keep warm.

Melt half the butter in a large saucepan. Add the cream and, when just coming to a boil, add the fontina, provolone, Gruyère, and blue castello cheeses, stirring constantly over low heat for 3 minutes or until melted. Season with salt and ground white pepper. Add the pasta to the cheese mixture and mix well.

Spoon the mixture into a greased, shallow, 8 cup, flameproof dish. Sprinkle with the bread crumbs mixed with the Parmesan, dot with the remaining cubed butter, and bake for 25 minutes or until the top is golden and crisp. Serve with a salad.

Serves 4

Osso buco with tomatoes

10 pieces veal shank, about 1 1/2 inch
   thick
all-purpose flour, seasoned with salt
   and pepper
1/4 cup olive oil
1/4 cup butter
1 garlic clove
1 small carrot, finely chopped
1 large onion, finely chopped
1/2 celery stalk, finely chopped
1 cup dry white wine
1 1/2 cups veal or chicken stock
14 oz. can diced tomatoes
bouquet garni

Tie each piece of veal shank around its girth to secure the flesh, then dust with the seasoned flour. Heat the oil, butter, and garlic in a large, heavy saucepan big enough to hold the shanks in a single layer. Put the shanks in the saucepan and cook for 12–15 minutes or until well browned. Remove the shanks from the saucepan and set aside. Discard the garlic.

Add the carrot, onion, and celery to the saucepan and cook over moderate heat for 5–6 minutes without browning. Increase the heat to high, add the wine, and cook for 2–3 minutes. Add the stock, tomatoes, and bouquet garni. Season with salt and pepper.

Return the veal shanks to the saucepan, standing them up in a single layer. Cover the saucepan, reduce the heat, and simmer for 1 hour or until the meat is tender and you can cut it with a fork.

If you prefer a thicker sauce, remove the veal shanks and increase the heat. Boil the sauce until reduced and thickened, then return the veal to the saucepan. Discard the bouquet garni and season to taste. If desired, serve with mashed potatoes.

Serves 4

Hoisin beef stew

1½ tablespoons peanut oil
2¼ lb. stewing beef (such as chuck),
   cut into 1¼ inch cubes
1 tablespoon finely chopped ginger
1 tablespoon finely chopped garlic
4 cups good-quality beef stock
⅓ cup Chinese rice wine
⅓ cup hoisin sauce
2 inch piece cassia bark
1 piece dried tangerine peel
1 star anise
1 teaspoon Szechuan peppercorns,
   lightly crushed
2 teaspoons light brown sugar
10 oz. daikon, cut into 1¼ inch
   chunks
3 scallions, cut into 1¼ inch pieces,
   plus extra, to garnish
¼ cup sliced bamboo shoots
a few drops sesame oil (optional)

Heat a wok until very hot, add the peanut oil, and swirl to coat the side. Stir-fry the beef in four batches for 1–2 minutes per batch or until the meat is browned all over. Remove from the wok.

Add the ginger and garlic to the wok and stir-fry for a few seconds. Add the stock, rice wine, hoisin sauce, cassia bark, tangerine peel, star anise, peppercorns, sugar, daikon, and 3½ cups water, then return the beef to the wok.

Bring to a boil, removing any foam that forms on the surface, then reduce to a simmer and cook, stirring occasionally, for 1½ hours or until the beef is tender and the sauce has thickened slightly. Add the scallions and bamboo shoots 5 minutes before the end of the cooking time. Stir in a few drops of sesame oil, if desired, and garnish with the extra scallions. Serve with rice.

Serves 6

Note: You can remove the star anise, cassia bark, and tangerine peel before serving or leave them in the serving dish for presentation.

Pork sausage, soybean, and tomato casserole

1½ cups dried soybeans, soaked in
   cold water for at least 8 hours or
   overnight
8 thin pork sausages (1¼ lb.)
2 tablespoons vegetable oil
1 red onion, chopped
4 garlic cloves, chopped
1 large carrot, diced
1 celery stalk, diced
2 x 14 oz. cans diced tomatoes
1 tablespoon tomato paste
1 cup white wine
2 thyme sprigs
1 teaspoon dried oregano leaves
1 tablespoon oregano, chopped

Drain the soybeans, place in a large saucepan, and cover with fresh water. Bring to a boil, then reduce the heat and slowly simmer for 1¼–2 hours— keep the beans covered with water during cooking. Drain. Prick the sausages all over and then cook in a frying pan for 10 minutes or until browned. Drain on paper towels.

Heat the oil in a 14 cup, flameproof casserole. Add the onion and garlic and cook over medium heat for 5 minutes. Add the carrot and celery. Cook, stirring, for 5 minutes. Stir in the tomatoes, tomato paste, wine, thyme, and dried oregano and bring to a boil. Reduce to a simmer, stirring often, for 10 minutes or until the liquid has reduced and thickened slightly.

Preheat the oven to 315°F. Add the sausages, beans, and 1 cup water to the casserole. Bake, covered, for 2 hours. Stir occasionally, adding more water if necessary to keep the beans just covered.

Return the dish to the heat, skim off any fat, then reduce the liquid until thickened slightly. Remove the thyme sprigs and stir in the oregano.

Serves 4

Slow-cooked lamb shanks with soft polenta

¼ cup olive oil
8 lamb shanks
¼ cup seasoned flour
2 onions, sliced
3 garlic cloves, crushed
1 celery stalk, cut into 1 inch pieces
2 long, thin carrots, cut into 1¼ inch chunks
2 parsnips, peeled and cut into 1¼ inch chunks
1 cup red wine
3 cups chicken stock
1 cup tomato passata (strained tomatoes)
1 bay leaf
1 thyme sprig, plus extra, to garnish
zest of half an orange (without pith), cut into thick strips
1 parsley sprig

Polenta
2 cups chicken stock
1 cup fine instant polenta (cornmeal)
¼ cup butter
pinch paprika, for sprinkling

Preheat the oven to 315°F. Heat the oil in a large, heavy-bottomed, flameproof casserole big enough to fit the shanks in a single layer. Lightly dust the shanks with seasoned flour, then brown them in batches on the stovetop. Remove from the dish. Add the onions, reduce the heat, and cook for 3 minutes. Stir in the garlic, celery, carrots, and parsnips, add the wine, and simmer for 1 minute, then return the shanks to the casserole. Add the stock, tomato passata, bay leaf, thyme, orange zest, and parsley. Cover and bake for 2 hours.

To make the polenta, place the stock and 2 cups water in a large saucepan and bring to a boil. Gradually stir in the polenta using a wooden spoon. Reduce the heat and simmer over low heat, stirring often, for 5–6 minutes or until the mixture thickens and starts to leave the side of the saucepan. Remove from the heat, stir in the butter, and season. Spoon into a warm dish and sprinkle with paprika.

Remove the shanks from the saucepan and arrange on a warm serving platter. Discard the herbs and zest, then spoon the vegetables and gravy over the shanks. Garnish with the thyme sprigs. Serve with the soft polenta.

Serves 4

Chicken casserole with mustard and tarragon

¼ cup olive oil
2¼ lb. boneless, skinless chicken
   thighs, halved, then quartered
1 onion, finely chopped
1 leek, sliced
1 garlic clove, finely chopped
¾ lb. button mushrooms, sliced
½ teaspoon dried tarragon
1½ cups chicken stock
¾ cup light whipping cream
2 teaspoons lemon juice
2 teaspoons Dijon mustard

Preheat the oven to 350°F. Heat 1 tablespoon of the oil in a flameproof casserole over medium heat and cook the chicken in two batches for 6–7 minutes each or until golden. Remove from the dish.

Add the remaining oil to the casserole and cook the onion, leek, and garlic over medium heat for 5 minutes or until soft. Add the mushrooms and cook for 5–7 minutes or until they are soft and browned and most of the liquid has evaporated. Add the tarragon, chicken stock, cream, lemon juice, and mustard, bring to a boil, and cook for 2 minutes. Return the chicken pieces to the casserole and season well. Cover.

Place the casserole in the oven and cook for 1 hour or until the sauce has reduced and thickened. Season with salt and pepper and serve with potatoes and a green salad.

Serves 4–6

Veal Marsala

4 pieces (1 lb.) veal schnitzel
all-purpose flour, seasoned
1/4 cup butter
1 tablespoon vegetable oil
3/4 cup dry Marsala
3 teaspoons light whipping cream
2 tablespoons butter, chopped, extra

Using a meat mallet or the heel of your hand, flatten the schnitzel pieces to 1/4 inch thick. Dust the veal in the flour, shaking off any excess. Heat the butter and oil in a large frying pan and cook the veal over medium-high heat for 1–2 minutes on each side or until almost cooked through. Remove and keep warm.

Add the Marsala to the pan and bring to a boil, scraping the bottom of the pan to loosen any sediment. Reduce the heat and simmer for 1–2 minutes or until slightly reduced. Add the cream and simmer for 2 minutes, then whisk in the extra butter until the sauce thickens slightly. Return the veal to the pan and simmer for 1 minute or until the meat is warmed through. Serve immediately. Delicious with creamy garlic mashed potatoes and a tossed green salad.

Serves 4

Note: Purchase veal that is pale in color and free of sinew. Sinew will make the meat tough.

Fried beef with potato, peas, and ginger

vegetable oil, for deep-frying
1 potato, cut into small cubes
1 inch piece of ginger
1 1/4 lb. rump steak, thinly sliced
3 garlic cloves, crushed
1 teaspoon ground black pepper
2 tablespoons vegetable oil, extra
2 onions, sliced in rings
1/4 cup beef stock
2 tablespoons tomato paste
1/2 tablespoon soy sauce
1 teaspoon chili powder
3 tablespoons lemon juice
3 tomatoes, chopped
1/3 cup fresh or frozen peas

Fill a deep, heavy-bottomed saucepan one-third full with oil and heat to 350°F or until a cube of bread dropped in the oil browns in 15 seconds. Deep-fry the potato cubes until golden brown. Drain on paper towels.

Pound the ginger using a mortar and pestle or grate with a fine grater into a bowl. Put the ginger into a piece of cheesecloth, twist it up tightly, and squeeze out all the juice (you will need about 1 tablespoon).

Put the steak in a bowl, add the garlic, pepper, and ginger juice, and toss well. Heat the oil and fry the beef quickly in batches over high heat. Keep each batch warm as you remove it. Reduce the heat, fry the onions until golden, then remove.

Put the stock, tomato paste, soy sauce, chili powder, and lemon juice in the saucepan and cook over medium heat until reduced. Add the fried onions, cook for 3 minutes, add the chopped tomatoes and the peas, then stir well and cook for 1 minute. Add the beef and potato and toss well until heated through.

Serves 4

Beef Stroganoff

14 oz. beef fillet, cut into
  2 x ½ inch strips
2 tablespoons all-purpose flour
¼ cup butter
1 onion, thinly sliced
1 garlic clove, crushed
½ lb. small portobello mushrooms,
  sliced
¼ cup brandy
1 cup beef stock
1½ tablespoons tomato paste
¾ cup sour cream
1 tablespoon chopped Italian parsley

Dust the beef strips in flour, shaking off any excess.

Melt half the butter in a large frying pan and cook the meat in small batches for 1–2 minutes or until seared all over. Remove. Add the remaining butter to the pan and cook the onion and garlic over medium heat for 2–3 minutes or until they soften. Add the mushrooms and cook for 2–3 minutes.

Pour in the brandy and simmer until nearly all of the liquid has evaporated, then stir in the beef stock and tomato paste. Cook for 5 minutes to reduce the liquid slightly. Return the beef strips to the pan with any juices and stir in the sour cream. Simmer for 1 minute or until the sauce thickens slightly. Season with salt and freshly ground black pepper.

Garnish with the chopped parsley and serve immediately with fettucine or steamed rice.

Serves 4

Irish stew

1 tablespoon butter
1 tablespoon vegetable oil
8 lamb shoulder chops, trimmed
4 slices bacon, cut into strips
1 teaspoon all-purpose flour
1 1/4 lb. potatoes, peeled and cut
   into thick slices
3 carrots, cut into thick slices
1 onion, cut into 16 wedges
1 small leek, cut into thick slices
1/4 lb. Savoy cabbage, thinly sliced
2 cups beef stock
2 tablespoons finely chopped
   Italian parsley

Heat the butter and oil in a flameproof casserole or a large, heavy-bottomed saucepan over high heat. Add the chops and cook for 1–2 minutes on each side or until browned, then remove from the dish. Add the bacon and cook for 2–3 minutes or until crisp. Remove with a slotted spoon, leaving the drippings in the dish.

Sprinkle the flour into the dish and stir to combine. Remove from the heat and layer half the potatoes, carrots, onion, leek, cabbage, and bacon in the bottom of the dish. Arrange the chops in a single layer over the bacon and cover with layers of the remaining vegetables and bacon.

Pour in enough of the stock to cover, then bring to a boil over high heat. Reduce the heat, cover, and simmer for 1 1/2 hours or until the meat is very tender and the sauce is slightly reduced. Season well with salt and freshly ground black pepper and serve sprinkled with the parsley.

Serves 4

Beef cooked in ragout

3¼ lb. piece of beef, such as top
   round or sirloin
¼ cup pork fat, cut into small, thin
   pieces
1½ tablespoons butter
3 tablespoons olive oil
pinch of cayenne pepper
2 garlic cloves, finely chopped
2 onions, finely chopped
2 carrots, finely chopped
1 celery stalk, finely chopped
½ red bell pepper, finely chopped
3 leeks, sliced
¾ cup red wine
1 tablespoon tomato purée or paste
1½ cups beef stock
¾ cup tomato passata (strained
   tomatoes)
8 basil leaves, torn into pieces
½ teaspoon finely chopped oregano
   leaves or ¼ teaspoon dried oregano
2 tablespoons finely chopped parsley
¼ cup heavy whipping cream

Make deep incisions all over the piece
of beef using the point of a sharp
knife, then push a piece of pork fat
into each incision.

Heat the butter and olive oil in a large
casserole dish and brown the beef for
10–12 minutes, until it is browned all
over. Season with salt and add the
cayenne, garlic, onions, carrots,
celery, pepper, and leeks. Cook over
moderate heat for 10 minutes, until
the vegetables are lightly browned.

Increase the heat, add the wine, and
boil until it has evaporated. Stir in the
tomato purée, then add the stock.
Simmer for 30 minutes. Add the
tomato passata, basil, and oregano
and season with pepper. Cover the
casserole dish and cook for 1 hour
or until the beef is tender.

Remove the beef from the dish and
allow to rest for 10 minutes before
carving. Season to taste and then
stir in the parsley and cream.

Serves 6

Note: This dish can be both appetizer
and main course in one pot. Serve
the ragout on spaghetti or bucatini
as a first course, and the beef with
vegetables or a salad for the entrée.

Curried sausages

9 thick beef or pork sausages
1 tablespoon vegetable oil
1 tablespoon butter
2 teaspoons grated ginger
3 garlic cloves, crushed
2 large onions, sliced
3 teaspoons curry powder
1 teaspoon garam masala
2 teaspoons tomato paste
1 tablespoon all-purpose flour
2½ cups hot chicken stock
2 bay leaves

Place the sausages in a saucepan, cover with cold water, and bring to a boil. Lower the heat and simmer for 3 minutes. Remove from the heat and allow the sausages to cool in the water, then drain, pat dry, and cut into ¾ inch pieces.

Heat the oil in a large frying pan over high heat and cook the sausages for 2–3 minutes or until golden all over. Drain on paper towels.

Using the same pan, melt the butter, then add the ginger, garlic, and onions. Cook over medium heat for about 5 minutes or until the onions are soft and golden. Add the curry powder and garam masala and cook for 1 minute or until fragrant. Stir in the tomato paste and cook for 1 minute, then add the flour. Stir to combine, then gradually pour in the stock, making sure that no lumps form. Bring to a simmer, add the bay leaves and the sausages, and cook over low heat for 15 minutes or until thickened. Season and serve with mashed potatoes.

Serves 6

Pasta

Pasta with tomato and basil sauce

1 lb. penne rigate
1/3 cup extra-virgin olive oil
4 garlic cloves, crushed
4 anchovy fillets, finely chopped
2 small red chilies, seeded and finely chopped
6 large, vine-ripened tomatoes, peeled, seeded, and diced
1/3 cup white wine
1 tablespoon tomato paste
2 teaspoons sugar
2 tablespoons finely chopped Italian parsley
3 tablespoons shredded basil

Cook the pasta in a saucepan of boiling, salted water until al dente. Drain well.

Meanwhile, heat the oil in a frying pan and cook the garlic for 30 seconds. Stir in the anchovies and chilies and cook for 30 seconds. Add the tomatoes and cook for 2 minutes over high heat. Add the wine, tomato paste, and sugar and simmer, covered, for 10 minutes or until thickened.

Toss the tomato sauce through the pasta with the herbs. Season and serve with grated Parmesan, if desired.

Serves 4

Genovese pesto sauce

Pesto
2 garlic cloves
$^1/_3$ cup pine nuts
4$^1/_2$ oz. basil, stems removed
$^2/_3$–$^3/_4$ cup extra-virgin olive oil
$^1/_2$ cup Parmesan cheese, finely
  grated, plus extra, to serve

1 lb. trenette or spaghetti (see Note)
6 oz. green beans, trimmed
6 oz. small potatoes, very thinly sliced

Put the garlic and pine nuts in a food processor and process until finely ground (or use a mortar and pestle). Add the basil and then drizzle in the olive oil a little at a time while pounding or processing. When you have a thick purée, stop adding the oil. Season and mix in the Parmesan.

Bring a large saucepan of salted water to a boil. Add the pasta, green beans, and potatoes, stirring well to prevent the pasta from sticking together. Cook until the pasta is al dente (the vegetables should be cooked by this time), then drain, reserving a little of the water.

Return the pasta and vegetables to the saucepan, add the pesto, and mix well. If necessary, add some of the reserved water to loosen the pasta. Season and serve immediately with the extra Parmesan.

Serves 4

Note: Traditionally, pesto sauce is served with trenette pasta, green beans, and potatoes, but you can leave out the vegetables if you prefer or use spaghetti.

Penne with mushroom and herb sauce

2 tablespoons olive oil
1 lb. button mushrooms, sliced
2 garlic cloves, crushed
2 teaspoons chopped marjoram
1/2 cup dry white wine
1/3 cup light whipping cream
13 oz. penne
1 tablespoon lemon juice
1 teaspoon finely grated lemon zest
2 tablespoons chopped parsley
1/2 cup grated Parmesan cheese

Heat the olive oil in a large, heavy-bottomed frying pan over high heat. Add the mushrooms and cook for 3 minutes, stirring constantly to prevent the mushrooms from burning. Add the garlic and marjoram and cook for another 2 minutes.

Add the white wine to the pan, reduce the heat, and simmer for 5 minutes or until nearly all the liquid has evaporated. Stir in the cream and cook over low heat for 5 minutes or until the sauce has thickened.

Meanwhile, cook the penne in a large saucepan of boiling water until al dente. Drain.

Add the lemon juice, zest, parsley, and half the Parmesan to the sauce. Season to taste with salt and freshly ground black pepper. Toss the penne through the sauce and sprinkle with the remaining Parmesan.

Serves 4

Ricotta agnolotti with salmon and capers

1/2 cup olive oil
3 1/2 oz. capers, patted dry
1 lb. salmon fillets, skin removed
1 1/2 lb. ricotta agnolotti
2/3 cup butter
1 1/2 teaspoons grated lemon zest
2 tablespoons lemon juice
3 tablespoons chopped parsley

Heat half the oil in a small frying pan and cook the capers over high heat for 3–4 minutes or until golden and crispy. Drain on paper towels.

Season the salmon on both sides with salt and pepper. Heat the remaining oil in a nonstick frying pan and cook the salmon for 2–3 minutes each side or until just cooked through but still pink in the center. Remove from the pan and keep warm. Gently break into flakes with your fingers, being careful to remove any bones.

Cook the pasta in a large saucepan of boiling water until al dente. Drain and return to the saucepan to keep warm. Heat the butter in a frying pan over low heat for 5 minutes or until golden. Add the lemon zest, lemon juice, and parsley. Top the pasta with the flaked salmon and pour the brown butter on top. Sprinkle with the capers and serve immediately.

Serves 4

Creamy tomato and shrimp pasta

14 oz. dried egg tagliatelle
1 tablespoon olive oil
3 garlic cloves, finely chopped
20 medium shrimp, peeled and
  deveined, with tails intact
1¼ lb. plum tomatoes, diced
2 tablespoons thinly sliced basil
½ cup white wine
⅓ cup light whipping cream
basil leaves, to garnish

Cook the pasta in a large saucepan of boiling water until al dente. Drain and keep warm, reserving 2 tablespoons of the cooking water.

Meanwhile, heat the oil and garlic in a large frying pan over low heat for 1–2 minutes. Increase the heat to medium, add the shrimp, and cook for 3–5 minutes, stirring frequently until cooked. Remove the shrimp and keep warm.

Add the tomatoes and sliced basil and stir for 3 minutes or until the tomatoes are soft. Pour in the wine and cream, bring to a boil, and simmer for 2 minutes.

Purée the sauce in a blender, return to the pan, then add the reserved pasta water and bring to a simmer. Stir in the shrimp until heated through. Toss through the pasta and serve garnished with the basil leaves.

Serves 4

Orecchiette with spiced squash and yogurt

2¼ lb. butternut squash, cut into ¾ inch cubes
⅓ cup olive oil
1 lb. orecchiette (see Note)
2 garlic cloves, crushed
1 teaspoon dried chili flakes
1 teaspoon coriander seeds, crushed
1 tablespoon cumin seeds, crushed
¾ cup plain yogurt
3 tablespoons chopped cilantro

Preheat the oven to 400°F. Toss the squash cubes in 2 tablespoons of the oil, place in a roasting pan, and cook for 30 minutes or until golden and crisp, tossing halfway through.

Meanwhile, cook the pasta in a large saucepan of boiling water until al dente. Drain and return to the saucepan.

Heat the remaining oil in a saucepan. Add the garlic, chili, coriander, and cumin and cook for 30 seconds or until fragrant. Toss the spice mix and squash through the pasta, then stir in the yogurt and cilantro and season to taste with salt and freshly ground black pepper. Divide among serving bowls.

Serves 6

Note: Orecchiette means "little ears" in Italian, and the name of the pasta is a literal description of the shape—although some brands look more like curls than ears. If unavailable, use conchiglie or cavatelli.

Tagliatelle with tuna, capers, and arugula

12 oz. fresh tagliatelle
3 garlic cloves, crushed
1 teaspoon finely grated lemon zest
1/3 cup extra-virgin olive oil
1 lb. tuna, cut into 1/2 inch cubes
4 1/2 cups arugula leaves, washed, dried, and roughly chopped
4 tablespoons baby capers in salt, rinsed and squeezed dry
1/4 cup lemon juice
2 tablespoons finely chopped Italian parsley

Cook the pasta in a saucepan of boiling water until al dente.

Meanwhile, put the garlic, lemon zest, and 1 tablespoon of the oil in a bowl with the tuna and gently mix. Season.

Heat a frying pan over high heat and sear the tuna for 30 seconds on each side. Add the arugula and capers and gently stir for 1 minute or until the arugula has just wilted. Pour in the lemon juice and then remove from the heat.

Add the remaining oil to the hot pasta along with the tuna mixture and parsley. Season to taste and gently toss. Serve immediately.

Serves 4

Pasta carbonara

14 oz. penne
1 tablespoon olive oil
7 oz. piece pancetta or bacon, cut
into long, thin strips
6 egg yolks
3/4 cup heavy whipping cream
3/4 cup grated Parmesan cheese

Cook the pasta in a saucepan of boiling water until al dente.

Meanwhile, heat the oil in a frying pan and cook the pancetta over high heat for 6 minutes or until crisp and golden. Remove with a slotted spoon and drain on paper towels.

Beat the egg yolks, cream, and the Parmesan together in a bowl and season generously. Return the freshly cooked and drained pasta to its saucepan and pour the egg mixture over the pasta, tossing gently. Add the pancetta, then return the saucepan to very low heat and cook for 30–60 seconds or until the sauce thickens and coats the pasta. Season with pepper and serve immediately.

Serves 4–6

Note: Be careful not to cook the pasta over high heat once you have added the egg mixture, or the sauce risks becoming scrambled by the heat.

Pasta with chicken, mushrooms, and tarragon

13 oz. fusilli or other pasta shapes
  such as ruote, conchiglie, or penne
2 tablespoons virgin olive oil
12 oz. chicken tenderloins, cut into
  3/4 inch pieces
1 tablespoon butter
1 lb. portobello or button mushrooms,
  sliced
2 garlic cloves, finely chopped
1/2 cup dry white wine
3/4 cup light whipping cream
1 teaspoon finely grated lemon zest
2 tablespoons lemon juice
1 tablespoon chopped tarragon
2 tablespoons chopped parsley
1/4 cup grated Parmesan cheese, plus
  extra, to serve

Cook the pasta in a large saucepan of boiling water until al dente.

Meanwhile, heat 1 tablespoon of the oil in a large frying pan, add the chicken, and cook over high heat for 3–4 minutes or until lightly browned. Remove from the saucepan.

Heat the butter and the remaining oil, add the mushrooms, and cook, stirring, over high heat for 3 minutes. Add the garlic and cook for another 2 minutes.

Pour in the wine, then reduce the heat to low and simmer for 5 minutes or until nearly evaporated. Add the cream and chicken and simmer for about 5 minutes or until thickened.

Stir the lemon zest, lemon juice, tarragon, parsley, and Parmesan into the sauce. Season with salt and pepper, then add the hot pasta, tossing until well combined. Serve with the extra Parmesan.

Serves 4

Pasta primavera

¼ lb. fava beans, fresh or frozen
8 asparagus spears, cut into short
   pieces
12 oz. fresh tagliatelle
¼ lb. green beans, cut into short
   pieces
¾ cup peas, fresh or frozen
1½ tablespoons butter
1 small fennel bulb, thinly sliced
1½ cups heavy whipping cream
2 tablespoons grated Parmesan
   cheese, plus extra, to serve

Bring a large saucepan of water to a boil. Add 1 teaspoon of salt, the fava beans, and asparagus and simmer for 3 minutes.

Remove the vegetables with a slotted spoon and set them aside. Add the tagliatelle to the saucepan and, when it has softened, stir in the beans and the peas (if you're using frozen peas, add them a few minutes later). Cook for about 4 minutes or until the pasta is al dente.

Meanwhile, heat the butter in a large frying pan. Add the fennel and cook over moderately low heat, without coloring, for 5 minutes. Add the cream, season with salt and pepper, and cook at a low simmer.

Peel the skins from the fava beans. Drain the pasta, green beans, and peas and add them to the frying pan. Add 2 tablespoons of Parmesan and the fava beans and asparagus. Toss lightly to coat. Serve immediately with extra Parmesan.

Serves 4

Penne with veal ragout

2 onions, sliced
2 bay leaves, crushed
3¼ lb. veal shin, cut into osso buco
   pieces (about 1½ inches thick)
1 cup red wine
2 x 14 oz. cans crushed tomatoes
1½ cups beef stock
2 teaspoons chopped rosemary
14 oz. penne
1 cup frozen peas

Preheat the oven to 425°F. Sprinkle the onions over the bottom of a large roasting pan, lightly spray with oil, and put the bay leaves and veal pieces on top. Season with salt and pepper. Roast for 10–15 minutes or until the veal is browned. Watch the onions to make sure that they don't burn.

Pour the wine over the veal and return to the oven for another 5 minutes. Reduce the oven to 350°F, remove the pan from the oven, and pour on the tomatoes, stock, and 1 teaspoon of the rosemary. Cover with aluminum foil and return to the oven. Cook for 2 hours or until the veal is starting to fall from the bone. Remove the foil and cook for another 15 minutes or until the meat loosens away from the bone and the liquid has evaporated slightly.

Cook the pasta in a large saucepan of boiling water until al dente. Meanwhile, remove the veal from the oven and cool slightly. Add the peas and remaining rosemary and cook over medium heat for 5 minutes or until the peas are cooked. Drain the pasta, divide among four bowls, and top with the ragout.

Serves 4

Pasta with lentils, winter vegetables, and thyme

4 cups chicken stock
1 lb. conchigliette (small shell pasta) or orecchiette
2 tablespoons olive oil
1 onion, chopped
2 carrots, diced
3 celery stalks, diced
3 garlic cloves, finely chopped
1 1/2 tablespoons chopped thyme
14 oz. cooked green lentils, or canned
virgin olive oil, to drizzle
grated Parmesan cheese, to serve (optional)

Boil the chicken stock in a large saucepan for 10 minutes or until reduced to 2 cups. Meanwhile, cook the pasta in a saucepan of boiling water until al dente.

Heat the oil in a large, deep frying pan. Add the onion, carrots, and celery and cook over medium heat for 10 minutes or until browned. Add 2 cloves of the garlic and 1 tablespoon of the thyme and cook for another minute. Pour in the stock, bring to a boil, and cook for 8 minutes or until reduced slightly and the vegetables are tender. Gently stir in the lentils until heated through.

Stir in the remaining garlic and thyme and season with plenty of salt and freshly ground black pepper—the stock should be slightly syrupy at this point. Combine the hot pasta with the lentil sauce in a large bowl, drizzle generously with the virgin olive oil, and serve with Parmesan, if desired.

Serves 4

Penne with meatballs and tomato sauce

Meatballs
2 slices white bread, crusts removed
1/4 cup milk
1 lb. ground pork and veal (see Note)
1 small onion, finely chopped
2 garlic cloves, finely chopped
3 tablespoons finely chopped Italian
  parsley
2 teaspoons finely grated lemon zest
1 egg, lightly beaten
1/2 cup grated Parmesan cheese
all-purpose flour, to coat
2 tablespoons olive oil

1/2 cup white wine
2 x 14 oz. cans diced tomatoes
1 tablespoon tomato paste
1 teaspoon superfine sugar
1/2 teaspoon dried oregano
1 lb. penne rigate (penne with ridges)
oregano leaves, to garnish

To make the meatballs, soak the bread in the milk for 5 minutes, then squeeze out any moisture. Put the bread, ground meat, onion, garlic, parsley, zest, egg, and Parmesan in a bowl, season, and mix well with your hands.

Shape into walnut-size balls using damp hands and roll lightly in the flour. Heat the oil in a large, deep frying pan and cook the meatballs in batches over medium heat, turning frequently, for 10 minutes or until brown all over. Remove with a slotted spoon and drain on paper towels.

Pour the wine into the same frying pan and boil over medium heat for 2–3 minutes or until it evaporates a little. Add the tomatoes, tomato paste, sugar, and dried oregano. Reduce the heat, then simmer for 20 minutes to thicken the sauce. Add the meatballs and simmer for 10 minutes. Meanwhile, cook the pasta in a saucepan of boiling water until al dente.

To serve, divide the hot pasta among six serving plates and spoon some meatballs and sauce over the top of each. Garnish with the oregano.

Serves 6

Note: Use ground beef instead of the pork and veal, if you prefer.

Spaghetti with anchovies, capers, and chili

14 oz. spaghettini (thin spaghetti)
1/2 cup olive oil
4 garlic cloves, finely chopped
10 anchovy fillets, chopped
1 tablespoon baby capers, rinsed and
  squeezed dry
1 teaspoon chili flakes
2 tablespoons lemon juice
2 teaspoons finely grated lemon zest
3 tablespoons chopped parsley
3 tablespoons chopped basil leaves
3 tablespoons chopped mint
1/2 cup coarsely grated Parmesan
  cheese, plus extra, to serve
extra-virgin olive oil, to drizzle

Cook the pasta in a saucepan of boiling water until al dente.

Heat the oil in a frying pan and cook the garlic over medium heat for 2–3 minutes or until starting to brown. Add the anchovies, capers, and chili and cook for 1 minute.

Add the hot pasta to the pan with the lemon juice, zest, parsley, basil, mint, and Parmesan. Season with salt and pepper and toss together well.

To serve, drizzle with a little extra oil and sprinkle with Parmesan.

Serves 4

Blue cheese and walnut lasagnette

13 oz. lasagna noodles
1 cup walnuts
3 tablespoons butter
3 shallots, finely chopped
1 tablespoon brandy or cognac
1 cup crème fraîche
7 oz. Gorgonzola cheese, crumbled
  (see Note)
1⅓ cups baby spinach leaves

Preheat the oven to 400°F. Cook the pasta in a large saucepan of boiling water until al dente. Drain, return to the saucepan, and keep warm.

Meanwhile, place the walnuts on a cookie sheet and roast for 5 minutes or until golden and toasted. Cool, then roughly chop.

Heat the butter in a large saucepan, add the shallots, and cook over medium heat for 1–2 minutes or until soft, being careful not to brown. Add the brandy and simmer for 1 minute, then stir in the crème fraîche and Gorgonzola. Cook for 3–4 minutes or until the cheese has melted and the sauce has thickened.

Stir in the spinach and toasted walnuts, reserving 1 tablespoon for garnish. Heat gently until the spinach has just wilted. Season with salt and cracked black pepper. Gently mix the sauce through the pasta. Divide among serving plates and sprinkle with the reserved walnuts.

Serves 4

Note: The Gorgonzola needs to be young, as this gives a sweeter, milder flavor to the sauce.

Pasta with grilled peppers

6 large red bell peppers, halved
14 oz. pasta gnocchi (see Note)
2 tablespoons olive oil
1 onion, thinly sliced
3 garlic cloves, finely chopped
2 tablespoons shredded basil leaves
whole basil leaves, to garnish
shaved Parmesan cheese, to serve

Cut the peppers into large, flattish pieces. Cook, skin side up, under a preheated broiler until the skin blackens and blisters. Place in a plastic bag and allow to cool, then peel the skin.

Cook the pasta in a saucepan of boiling water until al dente. Meanwhile, heat the oil in a large frying pan, add the onion and garlic, and cook over medium heat for 5 minutes or until soft. Cut one pepper into thin strips and add to the onion mixture.

Chop the remaining peppers, then purée in a food processor until smooth. Add to the onion mixture and cook over low heat for 5 minutes or until warmed through.

Toss the sauce through the hot pasta. Season, then stir in the shredded basil. Garnish with the basil leaves and serve with the Parmesan.

Serves 4–6

Note: Not to be confused with the potato dumplings of the same name, pasta gnocchi is, as the name suggests, similar in shape to potato gnocchi. If unavailable, use conchiglie or orecchiette.

Spaghetti vongole

2¼ lb. baby clams
13 oz. spaghetti
½ cup virgin olive oil
2 tablespoons butter
1 small onion, very finely chopped
6 large garlic cloves, finely chopped
½ cup dry white wine
1 small red chili, seeded and finely
  chopped
½ cup chopped Italian parsley

Scrub the clams with a small, stiff brush to remove any grit, discarding any that are open or cracked. Then soak and rinse the clams in several changes of water over an hour or so until the water is clean and free of grit. Drain and set aside.

Cook the pasta in a saucepan of boiling water until al dente.

Heat the oil and 1 tablespoon of the butter in a large saucepan over medium heat. Add the onion and half the garlic and cook for 10 minutes or until lightly golden—make sure the garlic doesn't start to burn. Add the wine and cook for 2 minutes. Add the clams, chili, and the remaining butter and garlic and cook, covered, for 8 minutes, shaking regularly, until the clams pop open—discard any that are still closed.

Stir in the parsley and season. Add the hot pasta and toss well.

Serves 4

Penne all'arrabbiata

2 tablespoons olive oil
2 large garlic cloves, thinly sliced
1–2 medium-size dried chilies
2 x 14 oz. cans tomatoes
14 oz. penne or rigatoni
1 basil sprig, torn into pieces

Heat the olive oil in a saucepan and add the garlic and chilies. Cook over low heat until the garlic is light golden brown. Turn the chilies over during cooking so both sides get a chance to infuse in the oil and turn slightly nutty in flavor. Add the tomatoes and season with salt. Cook gently, breaking up the tomatoes with a wooden spoon, for 20–30 minutes or until the sauce is rich and thick.

Meanwhile, cook the pasta in a large saucepan of boiling water until al dente. Drain.

Add the basil to the sauce and season just before serving, tossed with the pasta. If you prefer a hotter sauce, break open the chilies to release the seeds.

Serves 4

Pasta alla Norma

¾ cup olive oil
1 onion, finely chopped
2 garlic cloves, finely chopped
2 x 14 oz. cans chopped tomatoes
14 oz. bucatini or spaghetti
1 large eggplant (about 1 lb.)
½ cup basil leaves, torn, plus extra,
   to garnish
½ cup ricotta salata (see Note),
   crumbled
½ cup grated pecorino or Parmesan
   cheese
1 tablespoon extra-virgin olive oil, to
   drizzle

Heat 2 tablespoons of the oil in a frying pan and cook the onion over medium heat for 5 minutes or until softened. Stir in the garlic and cook for 30 seconds. Add the tomatoes and season. Reduce the heat to low and cook for 20–25 minutes or until the sauce has thickened and reduced.

Cook the pasta in a saucepan of boiling water until al dente. Meanwhile, cut the eggplant lengthwise into ¼ inch thick slices. Heat the remaining olive oil in a large frying pan. When the oil is hot but not smoking, add the eggplant slices a few at a time and cook for 3–5 minutes or until lightly browned on both sides. Remove from the pan and drain on crumpled paper towels.

Add the eggplant to the sauce with the basil, stirring over very low heat.

Add the hot pasta to the sauce with half each of the ricotta and pecorino and toss together well. Serve immediately, sprinkled with the remaining cheeses and extra basil and drizzled with oil.

Serves 4–6

Note: Ricotta salata is a lightly salted, pressed ricotta cheese. If unavailable, use a mild feta cheese.

Spaghetti marinara

1 lb. spaghetti
1 tablespoon olive oil
1 onion, finely chopped
3 garlic cloves, finely chopped
2 x 14 oz. cans chopped tomatoes
2 tablespoons tomato paste
2/3 cup dry white wine
2 teaspoons light brown sugar
1 teaspoon finely grated lemon zest
2 tablespoons torn basil leaves, plus
   extra, to garnish
2 tablespoons finely chopped Italian
   parsley
12 medium shrimp, peeled and
   deveined, with tails intact
8 black mussels, scrubbed and
   beards removed
8 large white scallops, without roe
2 small squid tubes, cleaned and cut
   into 1/2 inch rings

Cook the pasta in a saucepan of boiling water until al dente.

Meanwhile, heat the oil in a large saucepan, add the onion, and cook over medium heat for 5–8 minutes or until golden. Add the garlic, tomatoes, tomato paste, wine, sugar, lemon zest, 1 tablespoon of the basil, the parsley, and 1 cup water. Cook, stirring occasionally, for 1 hour or until sauce is reduced and thickened. Season.

Add the shrimp and mussels and cook for 1 minute, then add the scallops and cook for 2 minutes. Stir in the squid and cook for 1 minute more or until all the seafood is cooked through and tender.

Add the hot pasta to the sauce with the remaining basil and toss together until well combined. Serve.

Serves 4

Pasta with lamb shank, rosemary, and red wine ragout

1 1/2 tablespoons olive oil
1 large onion, finely chopped
1 large carrot, finely diced
2 celery stalks, finely diced
2 bay leaves
3 1/4 lb. lamb shanks, trimmed of excess fat
4 garlic cloves, finely chopped
1 tablespoon finely chopped rosemary
3 cups dry red wine
4 cups beef stock
2 cups tomato passata (strained tomatoes)
1/2 teaspoon finely grated lemon zest
1 lb. pappardelle or any ribbon-shaped pasta
Italian parsley leaves, to garnish

Heat 1 tablespoon of the oil in a large, deep saucepan. Add the onion, carrot, celery, and bay leaves and cook over medium heat, stirring often, for 10 minutes or until the onion is lightly browned. Remove from the saucepan. Heat a little more oil in the saucepan and cook the shanks in two batches, turning occasionally, for 15 minutes or until browned. Remove from the saucepan.

Add the garlic and rosemary to the saucepan and cook for 30 seconds or until lightly golden and fragrant. Return the vegetables to the saucepan, then stir in the wine, stock, passata, zest, and 1 cup water. Using a wooden spoon, scrape up any sediment stuck to the bottom of the saucepan. Add the shanks and bring to a boil, removing any foam that rises to the surface. Reduce the heat and simmer, uncovered, for 2 1/4 hours or until the lamb is very tender and the sauce is thick and glossy. Meanwhile, cook the pasta in a saucepan of boiling water until al dente.

Remove the shanks from the sauce and remove the meat from the bones using a fork and tongs. Return the meat to the sauce and stir to heat through. Season. Toss the hot pasta through the sauce. Serve with parsley.

Serves 6–8

Linguine with ham, artichoke, and lemon sauce

1 lb. fresh linguine
1 tablespoon butter
2 large garlic cloves, chopped
2/3 cup marinated artichokes, drained
  and quartered
5 oz. sliced ham, cut into strips
1 1/4 cups light whipping cream
2 teaspoons coarsely grated lemon
  zest
1/2 cup basil, torn
1/3 cup grated Parmesan cheese

Cook the pasta in a large saucepan of boiling water until al dente. Drain, then return to the saucepan.

Meanwhile, melt the butter in a large frying pan, add the garlic, and cook over medium heat for 1 minute or until fragrant. Add the artichokes and ham and cook for another 2 minutes.

Add the cream and zest, reduce the heat, and simmer for 5 minutes, gently breaking up the artichokes with a wooden spoon.

Pour the sauce over the pasta, then add the basil and Parmesan and toss well until the pasta is evenly coated. Divide among four serving plates and serve immediately.

Serves 4

Buckwheat pasta with cabbage, potatoes, and cheese sauce

³/₄ lb. Savoy cabbage, roughly
    chopped
6 oz. potatoes, cut into ³/₄ inch cubes
1 lb. buckwheat pasta (pizzoccheri)
4 tablespoons extra-virgin olive oil
1 small bunch sage, finely chopped
2 garlic cloves, finely chopped
2¹/₃ cups mixed cheeses (such as
    mascarpone, fontina, Taleggio, and
    Gorgonzola)
grated Parmesan cheese, to serve

Bring a large saucepan of salted water to a boil. Add the cabbage, potatoes, and the pasta and cook for 3–5 minutes or until the pasta and vegetables are cooked through. Drain, reserving about a cup of the cooking water.

Dry the saucepan, then add the olive oil and gently cook the sage and garlic for 1 minute. Add the mixed cheeses to the saucepan. Mix briefly, then add the pasta, cabbage, and potatoes. Season with salt and pepper.

Remove the saucepan from the heat and gently stir the mixture together, adding some of the reserved pasta water to loosen it up a little if necessary. Serve with Parmesan sprinkled over the top.

Serves 6

Note: Buckwheat pasta is called *pizzoccheri* in Italy. This type of pasta is popular in Valtellina, near the Swiss border, and is traditionally served with potatoes, cabbage, and cheese.

Ravioli with shrimp and creamy lime sauce

2½ tablespoons butter
4 garlic cloves, crushed
1¾ lb. medium shrimp, peeled and deveined
1½ tablespoons all-purpose flour
1½ cups fish stock
2 cups cream
5 kaffir lime leaves, shredded
1½ lb. seafood ravioli (see Note)
3 teaspoons fish sauce

Melt the butter in a large, deep frying pan and cook the garlic over medium heat for 1 minute. Add the shrimp and cook for 3–4 minutes or until they turn pink and are cooked through. Remove from the pan, leaving any juices in the pan. Add the flour and stir for 1 minute or until lightly golden. Gradually stir in the stock, then add the cream and lime leaves. Reduce the heat and simmer for 10 minutes or until slightly thickened.

Meanwhile, cook the pasta in a large saucepan of boiling water until al dente. Drain.

Stir the fish sauce through the cream sauce, add the shrimp, and stir until warmed through. Divide the pasta among four warm serving plates and spoon on the shrimp and sauce. Season with salt and cracked black pepper and serve.

Serves 4

Note: Look for seafood ravioli in specialty pasta shops and gourmet food stores. If unavailable, you can use ricotta ravioli instead—the flavors work well.

Pasta with squash and feta

2¼ lb. butternut squash, peeled and
  cut into ¾ inch chunks
1 red onion, thinly sliced
8 garlic cloves, unpeeled
1 tablespoon rosemary leaves
⅓ cup olive oil
14 oz. casserechi pasta or macaroni,
  gemelli, or other short pasta
7 oz. marinated feta cheese,
  crumbled
2 tablespoons grated Parmesan
  cheese
2 tablespoons finely chopped parsley

Preheat the oven to 400°F. Put the squash, onion, garlic, and rosemary in a roasting pan, then drizzle with 1 tablespoon of the oil. Season. Using your hands, rub the oil over all the ingredients until well coated. Roast for 30 minutes or until the squash is soft and starting to caramelize.

Cook the pasta in a saucepan of boiling water until al dente.

Squeeze the roasted garlic out of its skin and place it in a bowl with the remaining oil. Mash with a fork.

Add the garlic oil to the hot pasta, then add the remaining ingredients. Toss well and season.

Serves 4

Ham tortellini with nutty herb sauce

1 lb. ham and cheese tortellini
2 tablespoons butter
1 cup walnuts, chopped
2/3 cup pine nuts
2 tablespoons finely chopped Italian
  parsley
2 teaspoons chopped thyme
1/4 cup ricotta cheese
1/4 cup heavy whipping cream

Cook the pasta in a large saucepan of boiling water until al dente. Drain and return to the saucepan.

Meanwhile, heat the butter in a frying pan over medium heat until foaming. Add the walnuts and pine nuts and stir for 5 minutes or until golden brown. Add the parsley and thyme and season to taste.

Beat the ricotta and cream together. Add the nutty sauce to the pasta and toss. Divide among serving bowls and top with the ricotta cream.

Serves 4–6

Tagliatelle with shrimp and leek in saffron cream

2 tablespoons butter
1 small leek, julienned
4 garlic cloves, finely chopped
pinch of saffron threads
1/2 cup dry vermouth
1 cup fish stock
1 1/4 cups heavy whipping cream
14 oz. fresh tagliatelle or any long, flat pasta
24 medium shrimp, peeled and deveined, with tails intact
1 tablespoon lemon juice
1 tablespoon finely chopped chervil, plus extra, to garnish (see Variation)

Melt the butter in a saucepan over medium heat, add the leek and garlic, and cook for 5 minutes or until the leek is soft and translucent. Add the saffron, vermouth, and fish stock and bring to a boil, skimming off any foam that rises to the surface. Reduce the heat to low and simmer for 10 minutes or until the sauce has reduced by half. Pour in the cream and simmer for 15 minutes or until the sauce has thickened and reduced by about a third.

Meanwhile, cook the pasta in a saucepan of boiling water until al dente.

Add the shrimp to the sauce and simmer for 2–3 minutes or until cooked through. Remove from the heat and stir in the lemon juice and chervil. Season well, then toss through the hot pasta. Serve immediately, garnished with a little extra chervil, if desired.

Serves 4–6

Note: This creamy pasta is very rich and more suitable as an appetizer than as a main course.
Variation: Parsley or dill can be used in place of chervil.

Orecchiette with cauliflower, bacon, and pecorino

1³/₄ lb. cauliflower, cut into florets
1 lb. orecchiette (see Note)
¹/₂ cup olive oil, plus extra, to drizzle
5¹/₂ oz. bacon, diced
2 garlic cloves, finely chopped
¹/₂ cup pine nuts, toasted
¹/₂ cup grated pecorino cheese
¹/₂ cup chopped Italian parsley
³/₄ cup fresh bread crumbs, toasted

Bring a large saucepan of boiling water to a boil and cook the cauliflower for 5–6 minutes or until tender. Drain.

Cook the pasta in a large saucepan of boiling water until al dente.

Heat the oil in a frying pan and cook the bacon over medium heat for 4–5 minutes or until just crisp. Add the garlic and cook for 1 minute or until just beginning to turn golden. Add the cauliflower and toss well.

Add the cooked pasta to the pan with the pine nuts, pecorino cheese, parsley, and ¹/₂ cup of the bread crumbs and mix together. Season, sprinkle with the remaining bread crumbs, and drizzle with a little extra oil.

Serves 4

Note: Orecchiette means "little ears" in Italian, and the name of the pasta is a literal description of the shape—although some brands look more like curls than ears. If unavailable, use conchiglie or cavatelli.

Pasta amatriciana

2 tablespoons olive oil
7 oz. pancetta, thinly sliced
1 red onion, finely chopped
2 garlic cloves, finely chopped
1 teaspoon chili flakes
2 teaspoons finely chopped rosemary
2 x 14 oz. cans diced tomatoes
1 lb. bucatini or spaghetti
1/2 cup chopped Italian parsley

Heat the oil in a frying pan and cook the pancetta over medium heat for 6–8 minutes or until crisp. Add the onion, garlic, chili flakes, and chopped rosemary and cook for 4–5 minutes more or until the onion has softened.

Add the tomatoes to the pan, season with salt and pepper, and bring to a boil. Reduce the heat to low and simmer for 20 minutes or until the sauce is reduced and very thick.

Cook the pasta in a large saucepan of boiling water until al dente.

Toss the sauce with the hot pasta and parsley, then serve.

Serves 4

Veal tortellini with baked squash and basil butter

2¼ lb. butternut squash, cut into
  ¾ inch cubes
1¼ lb. veal tortellini
⅓ cup butter
3 garlic cloves, crushed
½ cup pine nuts
¾ cup firmly packed shredded basil
7 oz. feta cheese, crumbled

Preheat the oven to 425°F. Line a cookie sheet with waxed paper. Place the squash on the prepared cookie sheet and season well with salt and cracked black pepper. Bake for 30 minutes or until tender.

Meanwhile, cook the pasta in a large saucepan of boiling water until al dente. Drain and return to the saucepan.

Heat the butter over medium heat in a small frying pan until foaming. Add the garlic and pine nuts and cook for 3–5 minutes or until the nuts are starting to turn golden. Remove from the heat and add the basil. Toss the basil butter, squash, and feta through the cooked pasta and serve.

Serves 4

Pasta with roast chicken, pine nuts, and lemon

3 lb. whole chicken
1 garlic bulb, cloves separated and
  left unpeeled
¼ cup olive oil
2 tablespoons butter, softened
1 tablespoon finely chopped thyme
½ cup lemon juice
1 lb. bavette or spaghetti
2 tablespoons currants
1 teaspoon finely grated lemon zest
⅓ cup pine nuts, toasted
½ cup finely chopped Italian parsley

Preheat the oven to 400°F. Remove the neck from the inside of the chicken and place the neck in a roasting pan. Rinse the inside of the chicken with cold water and shake out any excess. Insert the garlic cloves into the cavity, then put the chicken in the roasting pan.

Combine the oil, butter, thyme, and lemon juice, then rub over the chicken. Season the chicken. Roast for 1 hour or until the skin is golden and the juices run clear when the thigh is pierced with a skewer. Transfer the chicken to a bowl to catch any juices while resting. Remove the garlic from the cavity, cool, then squeeze the garlic cloves out of their skins and finely chop.

Cook the pasta in a large saucepan of boiling water until al dente. Meanwhile, pour the juices from the roasting pan into a saucepan and discard the neck. Add the currants, zest, and chopped garlic, then simmer over low heat. Remove all the meat from the chicken and shred into bite-size pieces. Add the resting juices to the saucepan.

Add the chicken meat, pine nuts, parsley, and the sauce to the hot pasta and toss well. Season with salt and pepper and serve.

Serves 4–6

Pasta boscaiola

1½ tablespoons butter
4 slices bacon, diced
2 garlic cloves, finely chopped
¾ lb. portobello or button
  mushrooms, sliced
¼ cup dry white wine
1½ cups cream
1 teaspoon chopped thyme
1 lb. veal tortellini
½ cup grated Parmesan cheese
1 tablespoon chopped Italian parsley

Melt the butter in a large frying pan, add the bacon, and cook over medium heat for 5 minutes or until crisp. Add the garlic and cook for 2 minutes, then add the mushrooms, cooking for another 8 minutes or until softened.

Stir in the wine and cream, then add the thyme and bring to a boil. Reduce the heat to low and simmer for 10 minutes or until the sauce has thickened. Meanwhile, cook the pasta in a large saucepan of boiling water until al dente.

Combine the sauce with the pasta, Parmesan, and parsley. Season to taste and serve immediately.

Serves 4–6

Spaghettini with squid in black ink

2¼ lb. medium squid
2 tablespoons olive oil
1 onion, finely chopped
6 garlic cloves, finely chopped
1 bay leaf
1 small red chili, seeded and thinly
  sliced
⅓ cup white wine
⅓ cup dry vermouth
1 cup fish stock
¼ cup tomato paste
2 cups tomato passata (strained
  tomatoes)
½ oz. squid ink
1 lb. spaghettini
½ teaspoon Pernod (optional)
4 tablespoons chopped Italian parsley
1 garlic clove, extra, crushed

To clean the squid, pull the tentacles away from the hood (the intestines should come away at the same time). Remove the intestines by cutting under the eyes, and remove the beak by using your fingers to push up the center. Pull out the transparent quill from inside the body. Remove any white membrane. Cut the squid into thin slices.

Heat the oil in a saucepan over medium heat. Add the onion and cook until lightly golden. Add the garlic, bay leaf, and chili and cook for 2 minutes or until the garlic is lightly golden. Stir in the wine, vermouth, stock, tomato paste, passata, and 1 cup water, then increase the heat to high and bring to a boil. Reduce to a simmer and cook for 45 minutes or until the liquid has reduced by half. Add the squid ink and cook for 2 minutes or until the sauce is evenly black and glossy. Meanwhile, cook the pasta in a large saucepan of boiling water until al dente.

Add the squid rings and Pernod, stir well, then cook for 4–5 minutes or until the squid rings turn opaque and are cooked through. Stir in the parsley and the extra garlic and season. Toss through the pasta and serve.

Serves 4–6

Gnocchi with Gorgonzola cream

1 lb. store-bought potato gnocchi
walnuts, to garnish
1½ cups light whipping cream
7 oz. mild Gorgonzola cheese,
  crumbled
2 tablespoons grated Parmesan
  cheese
2 tablespoons butter
pinch of grated nutmeg

Cook the gnocchi in a large saucepan of boiling water until al dente.

Spread the walnuts on a baking tray and toast in a 350°F oven for 5–8 minutes or until lightly colored. Alternatively, place them on a cookie sheet under a preheated broiler. Once they start to brown, nuts burn very quickly, so watch them carefully. Cool, then roughly chop.

Put the cream, butter, Gorgonzola, and Parmesan in a saucepan and heat over low heat, stirring occasionally, for 3 minutes or until the cheeses have melted into a smooth sauce.

Stir in the nutmeg and serve immediately over the hot pasta. Garnish with the walnuts.

Serves 4–6

Note: This dish is very rich and is recommended as an appetizer rather than as a main course.

Tagliatelle with walnut sauce

2 cups shelled walnuts
1/3 cup roughly chopped parsley
2 1/2 tablespoons butter
3/4 cup extra-virgin olive oil
1 garlic clove, crushed
1/3 cup Parmesan cheese, grated
1/2 cup heavy whipping cream
14 oz. tagliatelle pasta

Dry-fry the walnuts over moderately high heat for 2 minutes or until browned. Set aside to cool for 5 minutes.

Put the walnuts in a food processor with the parsley and blend until finely chopped. Add the butter and mix together. Gradually pour in the olive oil in a steady stream with the motor running. Add the garlic, Parmesan, and cream. Season with salt and black pepper.

Cook the pasta in a large saucepan of boiling water until al dente. Drain, then toss through the sauce to serve.

Serves 4

Pasta bolognese

2 tablespoons olive oil
2 garlic cloves, finely chopped
1 large onion, finely chopped
1 carrot, finely chopped
1 celery stalk, finely chopped
1 3/4 oz. pancetta or bacon, finely
  chopped
1 lb. ground beef
2 cups beef stock
1 1/2 cups red wine
2 x 14 oz. cans diced tomatoes
2 tablespoons tomato paste
1 teaspoon sugar
1 lb. fresh tagliatelle (see Note)
shaved Parmesan cheese, to serve

Heat the oil in a large, deep saucepan. Add the garlic, onion, carrot, celery, and pancetta and cook, stirring, over medium heat for 5 minutes or until softened.

Add the ground beef and break up any lumps with the back of a spoon, stirring until just browned. Add the stock, red wine, tomatoes, tomato paste, and sugar. Bring to a boil, then reduce the heat to very low and simmer, covered, stirring occasionally, for 1 1/2 hours. Remove the lid and simmer, stirring occasionally, for another 1 1/2 hours. Season to taste with salt and freshly ground pepper. While the meat is cooking, cook the pasta in a saucepan of boiling water until al dente.

To serve, spoon the sauce over the hot pasta and sprinkle with some of the shaved Parmesan.

Serves 4–6

Note: Traditionally, bolognese was served with tagliatelle, but now we tend to serve it with spaghetti.

Spaghetti puttanesca

6 large, ripe tomatoes
13 oz. spaghetti
1/3 cup olive oil
2 onions, finely chopped
3 garlic cloves, finely chopped
1/2 teaspoon chili flakes
4 tablespoons capers, rinsed and
    squeezed dry
7–8 anchovies in oil, drained and
    chopped
5 1/2 oz. Kalamata olives
3 tablespoons chopped Italian parsley

Score a cross in the base of each tomato. Put the tomatoes in a bowl of boiling water for 30 seconds, then plunge into cold water and peel the skin away from the cross. Dice the tomato flesh. Cook the pasta in a large saucepan of boiling water until al dente.

Heat the oil in a saucepan, add the onions, and cook over medium heat for 5 minutes. Add the garlic and chili flakes and cook for 30 seconds before adding the capers, anchovies, and diced tomatoes. Simmer over low heat for 5–10 minutes or until thick and pulpy. Stir in the olives and parsley.

Add the hot pasta to the sauce and toss through until well combined. Season with salt and freshly ground black pepper and serve.

Serves 4

Pasta with artichokes and grilled chicken

1 tablespoon olive oil
3 boneless, skinless chicken breasts
1 lb. pasta, such as tagliatelle or any long, flat pasta
8 slices prosciutto
10 oz. jar artichokes in oil, drained and quartered, oil reserved
1 cup sun-dried tomatoes, thinly sliced
4 cups baby arugula leaves
2–3 tablespoons balsamic vinegar

Lightly brush a ridged grill pan or frying pan with oil and heat over high heat. Cook the chicken breasts for 6–8 minutes each side or until they are cooked through. Thinly slice and set aside.

Cook the pasta in a large saucepan of boiling water until al dente. Drain the pasta and return to the saucepan to keep warm. Meanwhile, place the prosciutto under a preheated broiler and broil for 2 minutes each side or until crisp. Cool slightly and break into pieces.

Combine the pasta with the chicken, prosciutto, artichokes, tomatoes, and arugula in a bowl and toss. Whisk together ¼ cup of the reserved artichoke oil and the balsamic vinegar and toss through the pasta mixture. Season and serve.

Serves 6

Pasta with creamy tomato and bacon sauce

14 oz. curly pasta such as cresti di
  gallo, cotelli, or fusilli (see Notes)
1 tablespoon olive oil
6 oz. bacon, thinly sliced
1 lb. plum tomatoes, roughly chopped
1/2 cup heavy whipping cream
2 tablespoons sun-dried tomato
  pesto
2 tablespoons finely chopped Italian
  parsley
1/2 cup finely grated Parmesan cheese

Cook the pasta in a large saucepan of boiling water until al dente. Drain and return to the saucepan.

Meanwhile, heat the oil in a frying pan, add the bacon, and cook over high heat for 2 minutes or until starting to brown. Reduce the heat to medium, add the tomatoes, and cook, stirring frequently, for 2 minutes or until the tomatoes have softened but still hold their shape.

Add the cream and tomato pesto and stir until heated through. Remove from the heat, add the parsley, and then toss the sauce through the pasta with the grated Parmesan.

Serves 4

Notes: Cresti di gallo pasta is named after the Italian word for "cockscomb" because of its similarity to the crest of a rooster.

Angel-hair pasta with scallops, arugula, and lemon

12 oz. angel-hair pasta
⅓ cup butter
3 garlic cloves, finely chopped
24 scallops, without roe
4 handfuls baby arugula leaves
2 teaspoons finely grated lemon zest
¼ cup lemon juice
¾ cup sun-dried tomatoes, thinly
  sliced

Cook the pasta in a large saucepan of boiling water until al dente.

Melt the butter in a small saucepan, add the garlic, and cook over low heat, stirring, for 1 minute. Remove the pan from the heat.

Heat a lightly greased, ridged grill pan over high heat. Lightly brush both sides of the scallops with the garlic butter and season with salt and pepper. When the grill pan is very hot, sear the scallops for 1 minute on each side or until golden and just cooked through. Keep warm.

Toss the hot pasta with the arugula, lemon zest and juice, tomato, and the remaining garlic butter until combined. Season. Divide among four bowls and top with the scallops.

Serves 4

Note: Put the scallops on to cook at the same time as the pasta.

Risoni risotto with mushrooms and pancetta

1 tablespoon butter
2 garlic cloves, finely chopped
5 oz. piece pancetta, diced
1 lb. button mushrooms, sliced
1 lb. risoni (rice-shaped pasta)
4 cups chicken stock
1/2 cup light whipping cream
1/2 cup finely grated Parmesan cheese
4 tablespoons finely chopped Italian
   parsley

Melt the butter in a saucepan, add the garlic, and cook over medium heat for 30 seconds, then increase the heat to high, add the pancetta, and cook for 3–5 minutes or until crisp. Add the mushrooms and cook for another 3–5 minutes or until softened.

Add the risoni, stir until it is coated in the mixture, then add the stock and bring to a boil. Reduce the heat to medium and cook, covered, for 15–20 minutes or until nearly all the liquid has evaporated and the risoni is tender.

Stir in the cream and cook, uncovered, for 3 minutes, stirring occasionally, until the cream is absorbed. Stir in 1/3 cup of the Parmesan and all the parsley and season with salt and cracked black pepper. Divide among four serving bowls and serve sprinkled with the remaining Parmesan.

Serves 4

Pasta gnocchi with sausage and tomato

1 lb. pasta gnocchi (see Note)
2 tablespoons olive oil
14 oz. thin Italian sausages
1 red onion, finely chopped
2 garlic cloves, finely chopped
2 x 14 oz. cans diced tomatoes
1 teaspoon superfine sugar
1/2 cup firmly packed basil, torn
1/2 cup grated pecorino cheese

Cook the pasta in a large saucepan of boiling water until al dente. Drain and return the pasta to the saucepan.

Heat 2 teaspoons of the oil in a large frying pan. Add the sausages and cook, turning, for 5 minutes or until browned and cooked through. Drain on paper towels, then slice when cool enough to touch. Keep warm.

Wipe clean the frying pan and heat the remaining oil. Add the onion and garlic and cook over medium heat for 2 minutes or until the onion has softened. Add the tomatoes, sugar, and 1 cup water and season well with cracked black pepper. Reduce the heat and simmer for 12 minutes or until thickened and reduced a little.

Pour the sauce over the cooked pasta and stir through the sausage, then the basil and half of the cheese. Divide among serving plates and serve hot with the remaining cheese sprinkled over the top.

Serves 4–6

Note: Not to be confused with the potato dumplings of the same name, pasta gnocchi is, as the name suggests, similar in shape to potato gnocchi. If unavailable, use conchiglie or orecchiette.

Tomato and ricotta orecchiette

14 oz. orecchiette, or conchiglie or
  cavatelli
1 lb. plum tomatoes
1 1/4 cups ricotta cheese
1 1/2 oz. Parmesan cheese, grated,
  plus extra, to serve
8 basil leaves, torn into pieces

Cook the pasta in a large saucepan of boiling water until al dente.

Score a cross in the top of each tomato, plunge them into boiling water (you can use the pasta water) for 20 seconds, then drain and peel the skin away from the cross. Core and chop the tomatoes. Mash the ricotta, then add the Parmesan and season with salt and freshly ground black pepper.

Drain the pasta and return to the saucepan. Add the ricotta mixture, the tomatoes, and the basil. Season and toss. Serve at once with the extra Parmesan.

Serves 4

Tagliatelle with salmon and creamy dill dressing

12 oz. fresh tagliatelle
1/4 cup olive oil
3 boneless, skinless salmon fillets
 (7 oz. each)
3 garlic cloves, crushed
1 1/2 cups light whipping cream
1 1/2 tablespoons chopped dill
1 teaspoon mustard powder
1 tablespoon lemon juice
1/3 cup shaved Parmesan cheese

Cook the pasta in a large saucepan of boiling water until al dente. Drain, then toss with 1 tablespoon of the oil.

Meanwhile, heat the remaining oil in a large, deep frying pan and cook the salmon for 2 minutes on each side or until crisp on the outside but still pink inside. Remove from the pan, cut into 3/4 inch cubes, and keep warm.

In the same pan, add the garlic and cook for 30 seconds or until fragrant. Add the cream, dill, and mustard powder, bring to a boil, then reduce the heat and simmer, stirring, for 4–5 minutes until thickened. Season.

Add the salmon and any juices, plus the lemon juice, to the creamy dill sauce and stir until warmed through. Gently toss the sauce and salmon through the pasta and divide among four serving bowls. Sprinkle with the Parmesan and serve.

Serves 4

Pasta pronto

2 tablespoons extra-virgin olive oil
4 garlic cloves, finely chopped
1 small red chili, finely chopped
3 x 14 oz. cans crushed tomatoes
1 teaspoon sugar
1/3 cup dry white wine
3 tablespoons chopped herbs such
   as basil or parsley
14 oz. vermicelli (see Note)
1/3 cup shaved Parmesan cheese

Heat the oil in a large, deep frying pan and cook the garlic and chili for 1 minute. Add the tomatoes, sugar, wine, herbs, and 1$3/4$ cups water. Bring to a boil and season.

Reduce the heat to medium and add the pasta, breaking the strands if they are too long. Cook for 10 minutes or until the pasta is cooked, stirring often to keep the pasta from sticking. The pasta will thicken the sauce as it cooks. Season to taste and serve in bowls with shaved Parmesan.

Serves 4

Note: Vermicelli is a pasta similar to spaghetti, but thinner. You can also use spaghettini or angel-hair pasta for this recipe.

Smoked salmon stracci in champagne sauce

13 oz. fresh stracci (see Notes)
1 tablespoon olive oil
2 large garlic cloves, crushed
½ cup champagne
1 cup heavy whipping cream
7 oz. smoked salmon, cut into thin
strips
2 tablespoons small capers in brine,
rinsed and patted dry
2 tablespoons chopped chives
2 tablespoons chopped dill

Cook the pasta in a large saucepan of boiling water until al dente. Drain and return to the saucepan.

Meanwhile, heat the oil in a large frying pan and cook the garlic over medium heat for 30 seconds. Pour in the champagne and cook for 2–3 minutes or until the liquid is reduced slightly. Add the cream and cook for 3–4 minutes or until the sauce has thickened.

Add the sauce, salmon, capers, and herbs to the hot pasta and toss gently. Season with salt and cracked black pepper and serve immediately.

Serves 4

Notes: Stracci is sold fresh and dried. Either is suitable for this recipe, or you can use fresh or dried fettucine or tagliatelle.
Dried lasagna sheets can also be used instead of stracci. Break them into ragged pieces measuring about 5 x 3 inches.

Index

Index

Index

Index

Photographers: Alan Benson, Cris Cordeiro, Craig Cranko, Joe Filshie, Jared Fowler, Ian Hofstetter, Chris L. Jones, Andre Martin, Jo Rankine, Rob Reichenfeld, Brett Stevens

Food Stylists: Marie-Hélène Clauzon, Jane Collins, Sarah de Nardi, Georgina Dolling, Carolyn Fienberg, Mary Harris, Katy Holder, Cherise Koch, Michelle Noerianto, Sarah O'Brien, Sally Parker

Food Preparation: Alison Adams, Rekha Arnott, Rebecca Clancy, Ross Dobson, Justin Finlay, Jo Glynn, Sonia Grieg, Valli Little, Ben Masters, Kerrie Mullins, Kate Murdoch, Briget Palmer, Kim Passenger, Justine Poole, Julie Ray, Christine Sheppard, Angela Tregonning

Laurel Glen Publishing
An imprint of the Advantage Publishers Group
5880 Oberlin Drive, San Diego, CA 92121-4794
www.laurelglenbooks.com

All notations of errors or omissions should be addressed to Laurel Glen Publishing, Editorial Department,
at the above address. All other correspondence (author inquiries, permissions, and rights) concerning the
content of this book should be addressed to Murdoch Books® a division of Murdoch Magazines Pty Ltd,
GPO Box 1203, Sydney NSW 2001, Australia.

NOTE: Those who might be at risk from the effects of salmonella poisoning (the elderly, pregnant women,
young children, and those with a compromised immune system) should consult their physician before
trying recipes made with raw eggs.

Library of Congress Cataloging-in-Publication Data

Comfort food
p.cm.
Includes index.
ISBN 1-59223-114-4
1. Quick and easy cookery.

TX833.5 .C63 2003
641.5'55--dc21   2003048762

Printed by Tien Wah Press, Singapore
2 3 4 5 6   08 07 06 05 04

Editorial Director: Diana Hill
Editors: Kim Rowney, Gordana Trifunovic
Creative Director: Marylouise Brammer
Designer: Michelle Cutler
Photographers (chapter openers): Jared Fowler, Alan Benson
Stylists (chapter openers): Cherise Koch, Katy Holder
Picture Librarians: Anne Ferrier, Tom Pender
Chief Executive: Juliet Rogers
Publisher: Kay Scarlett
Production: Janis Barbi

Front cover: Welsh lamb pie, page 258
Back cover: Ratatouille, page 257
Spine: Pasta with lamb shank, rosemary, and red wine ragout, page 343